SERVANT GLADLY:
ESSAYS IN HONOR OF
JOHN W. BEARDSLEE III

edited by
Jack D. Klunder
and
Russell L. Gasero

The Historical Series of the Reformed Church
in America

No. 19

Servant Gladly
Essays in Honor of
John W. Beardslee III

edited by
Jack D. Klunder
and
Russell L. Gasero

Wm. B. Eerdmans Publishing Co.
Grand Rapids, Michigan

Copyright © 1989 by Wm. B. Eerdmans Publishing Co.
255 Jefferson Ave. SE, Grand Rapids, Michigan 49503

Printed in the United States of America

Library of Congress Cataloging-in-Publication Data

Servant gladly: essays in honor of John W. Beardslee III /
  edited by Jack D. Klunder.
       p.   cm. — (The Historical series of the Reformed Church
  in America; no. 19)
    Bibliography: p. 117.
    Includes indexes.
    ISBN 0-8028-0466-7
    1. Reformed Church in America.   2. Reformed Church.   3. Beardslee,
John W., 1914–   .   I. Beardslee, John W., 1914–   .   II. Klunder,
Jack D.   III. Series.
BX9515.S47   1989
285.7′32—dc19   89-30640
                                         CIP

To
John W. Beardslee III
Teacher, Colleague, Pastor, Friend

The Historical Series of the Reformed Church in America

This series has been inaugurated by the General Synod of the Reformed Church in America, acting through its Commission on History, for the purpose of encouraging historical research and providing a medium wherein this knowledge may be shared with the academic community and with the members of the denomination in order that a knowledge of the past may contribute to right action in the present.

General Editor

The Rev. Donald J. Bruggink, Ph.D.
Western Theological Seminary

Commission on History

The Rev. Benjamin Alicea, Ph.D., Spotswood, New Jersey
The Rev. John Arnone, Ph.D., High Bridge, New Jersey
Professor Gerald F. DeJong, Ph.D., Orange City, Iowa
Glenna Foster, Union City, California
Professor Earl Wm. Kennedy, Th.D., Northwestern College
The Rev. Edwin G. Mulder, D.D., General Secretary,
        Reformed Church in America
The Rev. Dennis Voskuil, Ph.D., Hope College

The Writers

The Rev. James W. Van Hoeven, Ph.D., World Alliance of Reformed Churches, Dept. of Justice, Peace, and the Integrity of Creation

The Rev. Marion de Velder, D.D., General Secretary Emeritus, Reformed Church in America

The Rev. Arie R. Brouwer, D.D., General Secretary, National Council of Churches

The Rev. John Hubers, Missionary Pastor, Salallah, Oman

The Rev. Jack D. Klunder, Th.D., Pastor, The Church of the Good Shepherd, Franklin, Tennessee

Russell L. Gasero, Archivist, Reformed Church in America

The Rev. Elton J. Bruins, Ph.D., Evert J. and Hattie E. Blekkink Professor of Religion, Hope College

Professor Earl Wm. Kennedy, Th.D., Professor of Religion, Northwestern College

Greetings from New Brunswick Theological Seminary

A TRIBUTE TO JOHN W. BEARDSLEE III

The faculty and students of New Brunswick Theological Seminary join the authors of this Festschrift in expressing esteem and affection for Professor John W. Beardslee III, distinguished minister, scholar, and doctor of the Reformed Church in America. The Beardslee name has been spoken with honor in New Brunswick for more than a century. Like his father and grandfather before him, John W. Beardslee III is a man of extraordinary faith and learning. His ministry to students, colleagues, and the larger church has equipped another generation of informed and committed church leaders.

John Beardslee is a scholar steeped in the history of the church and shaped by the Reformed tradition. A man of deep and broad intellect, he has helped us to know ourselves by knowing our tradition and appropriating it critically and creatively for our time. Never the narrow antiquarian, John Beardslee is adept at reading the signs of the times. Like the prophets of old, his knowledge of God's mighty acts in history compel him to call for the church's witness to the righteousness of God here and now. Whether lecturing to students on Reformation history, addressing the General Synod on an issue of social justice, or protesting this nation's latest military misadventure, John Beardslee embodies that Reformed tradition which seeks nothing less than the transformation of persons and society according to the Word for the glory of God.

The vigor of John Beardslee's intellect and ministry have not diminished in retirement. As professor emeritus, he now shares time and wisdom freely with students and faculty at the seminary and as acting librarian at his beloved Gardner A. Sage Library. We are grateful for his daily presence. John is a rare man who observes St. Paul's dictum almost to a fault. He tends to think of himself less highly than he ought to think! That's reason all the more for us to honor John W. Beardslee III as he deserves and to thank almighty God for this gifted, humble teacher of the church in whom our best tradition lives.

Robert A. White
President

Greetings from Central College
Pella, Iowa

Dear John,

In the course of my long involvement with the educational institutions of the RCA I have come to a gradual but powerful conviction of the fundamental accuracy of the oft-cited but rarely examined assertion that an institution takes on the strengths of the people who have served it over the years.

Without question the denomination in general, and Central College in particular, have a deep thread of sensitivity to the social implications of the gospel which are reflective of your interest, your persistence, and your personal commitment.

We are the better for it. We thank you sincerely and take great pleasure in joining in this special tribute arranged by your students.

Sincerely,

Kenneth J. Weller
President

This volume is published with the assistance of many friends of John W. Beardslee III. The following organizations and individuals have helped to underwrite the expense of its publication. It is presented with gratitude and appreciation to John, our teacher, colleague, pastor, and friend.

Central College
Commission on History,
    Reformed Church in
    America
Historical Society of the
    Reformed Church in
    America
Benjamin Alicea
Harry J. Almond
David R. Armstrong
Charles R. Ausherman
William and Carolyn Babinsky
Rev. Robert W. Barrowclough
William A. Beardslee
Mary Belasco
Richard D. Beving
Robert J. Block
Donald A. Brevet
Arie R. Brouwer
David Lee Brower
Donald J. Bruggink
Elton J. Bruins
Eltje Brunemeyer
Rev. Barbara Dickens Burke
Alvin Cason
Mrs. Helen Clement
John Coakley
James I. Cook
David G. Corlett
Newton M. Coughenour
Jamie Daley
Harold L. Delhagen
John De Velder
Marion and Edith de Velder
S. William Duitsman
J. Dean Dykstra

James P. Ebbers
James C. Eelman
William E. Faulkner
Douglas W. Fromm, Jr.
Russell L. Gasero
Robert L. Gram
Howard G. Hageman
William L. Hanousek
Herman Harmelink III
John Hart
I. John Hesselink
John E. Hiemstra
L'Anni and William Hill-Alto
Jon Hinkamp
Martin Hoeksema
Marvin D. Hoff
Craig and Jan Hoffman
Renee S. House
John Hubers
Robert W. Jackson
Debra L. Jameson
Klaire Miller Jameson
David W. Jenks
William C. Johnson
David and Nancy Jones
David Jurgens
Leonard V. Kalkwarf
Earl Wm. Kennedy
Lee Kester, Jr.
Jack D. Klunder
Hugh Koops
Vernon and Margot Kooy
Ralph G. Korteling
Will Kroon
Herman E. Luben
John L. Magee, Jr.

Ebenezer Mane
Beth E. Marcus
Robert T. Marsh
Edward W. Meury
Alberta Meyer
Nickolas M. Miles
Mr. and Mrs. William H. Miles
Frederick Mold, Jr.
Kirk Moll
Paul and Laura Moyer
Richard Muenger
John Muilenburg
J. David Muyskens
Vernon O. Nagel
James Z. Nettinga
New Brunswick Theological
    Seminary
Leroy Nixon
Edwin F. Parsil
Russell F. Pater
Peter and Diana Paulsen
Bruce E. Penn
Raymond J. Pontier
Francis E. Potter
Linda S. Powell
Eugene E. Roberts
Gordon L. Robinson
Phyllis Jones Robinson
Robert W. Robinson
Garrett C. Roorda
Eileen L. Rosfjord
Anne Van Dillen Roth
J. Coert Rylaarsdam
Alyle A. Schutter
John H. Sharpe
Peter J. Shortway

Albert Smith
Charles R. Smyth
R. Smyth
F. Hugh Spencer
Louis O. Springsteen
Richard M. Suffern
Miklos Szolga
Paul M. Tanis II
John W. TerLouw
Norman E. Thomas
Walter Tsang
Gerard Van Dyk
Charles and Jean Van Engen
James W. Van Hoeven
Glenn Van Oort
George B. Van Pelt, Jr.
Gordon J. Van Wyk
Harold J. Vande Berg
James L. and Kathleen R.
    VandeBerg
Gerald L. Vermilyea
Frank Villerius
Harold and Neva Vogelaar
Jay Vogelaar
John H. Vruwink
David W. Waanders
Paul J. Walther
Barbara Walvoord
Dudley Webb
John C. White
Robert A. White
Arlene R. Wilhelm
G. J. Wullschleger
Everett L. Zabriskie III
Conley A. Zomermaand

Contents

Foreword

Servant Gladly is an appropriate title for a volume honoring Professor John W. Beardslee III. For more than four decades he has served with distinction the Reformed Church in America as pastor, missionary, ecumenist, teacher, prophet, consultant, archivist, theologian, historian, and much more. Few people in the long history of the Reformed Church can equal Professor Beardslee's influence or accomplishments. His students serve throughout the church, and their numbers are legion. His scholarly publications have rightly given him a worldwide reputation in academia, while also giving shape and direction to the church he loves.

Professor Beardslee's influence, however, transcends his considerable scholarly achievements. He is servant of the gospel, which in his case means a stranger in the world, a person never really at home in it, and at the same time a realist. It probably would have been easy for him to conform, for he knows the world well; it would have been easier for him to escape, and on more than one occasion he has told me he longed to retreat—to the sea, maybe, or to some utopianism, or to an "ivory tower" where he could research and write his books. God claimed him for another way to be, however, and his life is a witness to a decision never to conform and never to escape, which is another way of saying his life is a witness to courage in the world, for the sake of the gospel.

Thus it is that Professor Beardslee often left his study to march, demonstrate, speak-out, sit-in, or in a variety of other ways to do his part for peace and justice—in, for example, the anti-Vietnam War movement, nuclear disarmament, women's rights, and specifically women's ordination in the Reformed Church, minority rights in work, housing, and the voting booth, Jewish-Christian-Muslim conversation, and the committee for a Free South Africa. He participated in and championed these and other causes, while still finding time to be pastor and confidant to students and clergy, research, write and teach courses in theological history, and serve the church and seminary on a variety of boards, committees, commissions, and agencies. In short, Professor Beardslee possesses the rare gift that combines rigorous and careful scholarship with an equally rigorous and caring sensitivity to the rights of the human person. As such, he became one of the significant movers and shakers of the Reformed Church in America during the last half of the twentieth century.

The essays in this volume address a broad range of topics that have occupied the mind and soul of Professor Beardslee during his career. Appropriately, the first chapter is written by Marion de Velder, former general secretary of the Reformed Church in America, who provides a friend's-eye view of Professor Beardslee, including especially his nurturing in a distinguished family. The reader will warm to the many affectionate reminiscences in this essay—the classroom mannerisms, erudition, and leadership qualities of Beardslee's father, Dr. John W. Beardslee, Jr., who was professor of New Testament and president at New Brunswick Seminary from 1917 to 1949, the charm, insightfulness, and social activism of Beardslee's mother, "fearless Frances," who was known as the "loving arm" of the seminary student body, the precociousness of the five Beardslee children, including John W. III, each of whom was "one of those six going on sixteen prodigies," and the various vignettes that tell of the faith, love, and generous spirit of the Beardslee household, grounded in their profound devotion to God and the church, made strong by grace—all of which helped shape the life and faith of John W. III.

The remaining six chapters of the book are scholarly essays on topics of great interest to Dr. Beardslee, and to which he also has given witness and wisdom through his life and writing. Arie Brouwer's essay (chapter 2) sketches some of the checkered tradition of "advocacy for social justice in the Reformed Church in America," and challenges the reader toward ways of nurturing and renewing that tradition in order to bear faithful witness to the gospel in the face of the great social issues in the nation and in our global village. "Reformed Perspectives on War and Peace" (by John Hubers, chapter 3) and "A History of Synodical Opposition to the Heresy of Apartheid: 1952-1982" (by Jack Klunder, chapter 4) examine the history of Reformed Church confessional statements regarding two of the most critical issues of our age, namely, the Christian's response to the issue of war—particularly nuclear war, and the issue of apartheid in South Africa. The reader may be surprised by the volume of statements the Reformed Church has made on these systemic issues, and also by the writers' critiques of these statements.

The chapter (5) by Russell Gasero examines the process by which the Reformed Church established a theological library at New Brunswick. This essay is worth the price of the book, not only because it provides fresh information on this topic, but also because it underscores the importance of a few determined men and women of vision in getting things accomplished in the church. One would have thought a denomination with a historic commitment to education would make the development of a library a top priority issue. Not so, writes Gasero. That process was long, complex, and difficult, and had not "the right person been around at the right time" to champion the idea, or give sacrificially to it, there would be no library at New Brunswick today. Gasero's listing of some of the library's rare manuscript collections suggests that New Brunswick could well be a major center for theological research, and confirms that the library is one of the rich treasures of the Reformed Church in America.

At this point the book shifts to more traditional academic topics. Elton Bruins (chapter 6) narrates the rise and development of the reformed tradition in the Netherlands, 1560-1900, and shows the connection between that story and the formation of the Reformed and Christian Reformed churches in America. Those readers unfamiliar with this history will find this essay an excellent overview of the theological roots, piety, doctrinal quarrels, political battles, and confessional affirmations of the Reformed Church, from Calvin in the sixteenth century to the Abraham Kuyper and Albertus Van Raalte era in the nineteenth century.

Earl Kennedy's article compares and contrasts the eschatology of Francis Turretin and Charles Hodge (chapter 7). That Professor Beardslee's doctoral work focused on the orthodox formulations of Francis Turretin makes this essay particularly appropriate in this volume. The essay is even more appropriate, however, because both Turretin and Hodge significantly influenced the shape of piety and orthodoxy in the Reformed Church in the nineteenth century. The issue of general versus special grace is in this chapter, as are the issues relating to the doctrines of election and a pre-post-millennialism, all of which remind the reader of great battles in Reformed theology in the past. Kennedy gives spark to the chapter by drawing out the relevant questions for contemporary Reformed

Christians: 1) the impact of context on one's interpretation of Scripture, 2) the issue of the developmental nature of Christian theology, and 3) the relationship between eschatology and Christian social witness.

In 1964, I succeeded Professor Beardslee as teacher in the religion department at Central College, Pella, Iowa, where he had served for thirteen years (no one could have replaced him!). It was my first college teaching experience. Before the launching of that fall semester, Professor Beardslee called me with congratulations and this word of counsel: "Love your students as your friends," he said, "and the rest will be easy for you." I quickly learned that was good advice, just as I also learned that Professor Beardslee's students at Central College loved him as a friend, even as they admired his erudition and commitment to Christian social witness. Through the years since that time I have had numerous occasions to work with Professor Beardslee on boards, commissions, and various writing assignments for the church. In each case his insights, information, and wise counsel, always presented with characteristic humility, influenced my understanding of the subject, even as he influenced the life of the Reformed Church.

This small volume is a well-written tribute to Professor Beardslee, touching on topics to which he has devoted his life. His many students will rightly be moved by this tribute, and all of us will be informed, challenged, or inspired by it. So, begin the reading of these pages, and be grateful for the work and witness of our friend, Professor John W. Beardslee III, who in countless ways continues to serve gladly the church he loves.

James W. Van Hoeven

I

Recollections of the Beardslee Family

Marion de Velder

My First Beardslee

My first encounter with a Beardslee was in September of 1934, when I arrived as a junior student at New Brunswick Theological Seminary. I watched a medium-sized man, walking briskly with purpose across the campus, seemingly at home in the world. He moved composed and assured, as on a mission. Immaculately groomed, he wore a double-breasted gray tweed suit with wide-cuffed trousers, and highly polished shoes. Hatless and no overcoat—students said there was no evidence that he owned either. His appearance caught attention—a finely modeled head, high forehead and sparse hair, gold-rimmed glasses, all of which conveyed alertness and intelligence. Later I noted his graceful, mobile hands, penetrating yet loving eyes, the dimple in his chin, and a smile usually hovering around the left corner of his mouth. My senior fellow students told me he was Dr. John W. Beardslee, Jr., professor of New Testament studies and just appointed acting president of the seminary. He was fifty-five then, father of four sons and one daughter, devoted to the seminary, and known as a teacher unequaled, a man to be reckoned with.

Professor

In his classroom we learned rapidly and thoroughly. He was punctual, opening and closing each class exactly on time. Every moment was precious, with little time for small talk or banter. He believed in fresh air—a classroom window was always open, during fall, winter, spring. In his teaching, he was direct, precise, concise, with a no-nonsense mood, without patience for excess verbiage or tolerance for bluffing. His style was provocative and arresting, so there was no time for boredom or mind-wandering. His expositions of Scripture were vivid, his insights into the gospel penetrating, and his questions unusual and stimulating. Dr. Beardslee did not assume (though we were college graduates) that we knew how to use a library. So, early on, we were walked through Gardner Sage Library (his pride and joy), with instructions and suggestions for reading and research. I recall his course on the parables of Jesus. A description of his message goes something like this: Now, get the exact point Jesus made in the parable and stick to that point. Try to understand the point, making it as clear as possible to yourself and to others. When you get the specific meaning, don't qualify or condition the point. Jesus didn't stand on one foot and then the other. Don't worry about being one-sided. (If Jesus didn't worry about it, why should you?) There will always be another time to make another point. He shared with us his "paraphrases" of New Testament books, on which he had worked many hours over many years. He declined to call them "translations," for he was searching out the deeper meaning rather than trying to translate the words. His paraphrases sparked more insights and enlightened meanings than any exact translation ever could. He loved teaching, but loved his students more, developing into a trusted friend to each one. He gave generous, individual attention, ever confident that he would find a diamond in the rough. In our class of 1937 we had a great advantage: an ideal teacher-student ratio, as a small "Depression Era" class. Starting out with seven, we graduated as a class of four.

President

For twelve years, from 1935 to 1947, John W. Beardslee, Jr., served as president of New Brunswick Theological Seminary, in addition to his full load as professor. His term was marked by the dislocations of the Great Depression and World War II, often plagued with inadequate finances and small student bodies. Throughout, Beardslee worked with patience, tireless and painstaking in his planning to maintain academic excellence with competent faculty and visiting scholars. During this time the American Association of Theological Schools accredited the seminary as Class A "without notation," the highest rating available.

Scholar and Contributor

Overloaded, serving as president as well as full professor, Beardslee found it impossible to do personal research or publish his own work. However, he did serve as a consulting editor and as contributor to the monumental work, *The Interpreter's Bible,* and as a consultant for the Revised Standard Version of the Bible. His delight and love, though, was teaching, and he gave so much energy to it that he had little left for his own personal scholarship. An excellent explanation is found in a Memorial Resolution for Beardslee by the General Synod of 1962:

> The reticence and humility that often characterize great scholars together with a passion for meticulous accuracy restrained him from committing his work to print. But in the intimate fraternity of Biblical scholars he was recognized for his ripe scholarship, the integrity of his judgment and his profound knowledge of the intellectual climate of the Greco-Roman world which knew the visitation of the Gospel in the First Century.
>
> Minutes, General Synod, 1962, p. 36

An Unusual Tribute

In the summer of 1945 when I attended the University of Chicago Divinity School, I took a course in "Interpretation of the Gospel of John." The professor was Dr. Ernest C. Colwell, a noted authority on the Gospel of John, who continued to teach this course even though he was also the president of the university. Once he asked me about my seminary. When I told him that John W. Beardslee, Jr., had been my New Testament professor, he exclaimed, "Well! You were mighty fortunate. In my estimation, John Beardslee is one of the finest New Testament scholars and interpreters I know—in the class of Edgar J. Goodspeed!"

"Those Married Students"

In the middle 1930s married students were a novelty at New Brunswick Seminary. It was known that the outgoing president, William Henry Steele Demarest, frowned upon married students. He was a renowned and confirmed bachelor. At seventy-two, he had been president of Rutgers University from 1906 to 1924 and of

New Brunswick Seminary from 1925 to 1935, and had not dealt with married students during his career. An interchange was reported from a Board of Superintendents meeting in 1935, between President Demarest and the Reverend Jasper Hogan, minister of First Reformed Church of New Brunswick and a member of the board. In his annual report Demarest made an admission that, much to his surprise, he had noticed the superior academic work the married students were doing. Perhaps, he speculated, because married students were better motivated, had fewer distractions, stayed at home more, and could enjoy a settled home life. He appeared ready, it seemed, at this late stage in his life, to revise his thinking about married students in the seminary. During discussion of the report, Jasper Hogan wryly remarked, "Regarding brother Demarest's revised judgment about married students, isn't it too bad that he has realized this so late in life?" Whereupon Demarest rose to his feet, saying slowly, "Don't be so sure, Jasper. Perhaps it is not too late!" The new president, John W. Beardslee, Jr., a family-oriented man and father of five lively children, was always generous in his attitudes toward "those married students," eager also to help the wives in preparation for life in the manse.

Frances Davis Beardslee

Everyone knew that the Beardslee family of seven revolved around Frances Beardslee (President Beardslee's wife). She was a born general manager and presided over her home like a queen. A farm girl from just outside of Muscatine, Iowa, Frances Davis graduated from Wellesley with a M.A. She later pursued graduate studies in Greek literature at the University of Chicago and read Greek with her husband and sons. Three recollections of Frances Beardslee stand out:

Caring Friend

We remember her as a frequent caller in our seminary apartment in the (then) Van Dyke House, at 564 George Street. In our middle year there, my wife Edith was ill for a number of weeks with food poisoning from a below standard hamburger eaten in a Bayonne diner. Frances Beardslee came to visit frequently, to help, encourage, counsel, compliment, and inspire. We knew her as the "loving arm" of the seminary family.

Dinner at the Beardslees

Enjoying dinner in the Beardslee home was a seminary highlight for us. On one such occasion, after we had finished our soup and salad, the main course was brought in—a beautiful crown roast of lamb on a large silver platter. Placed in front of Professor Beardslee, it was a magnificent work of art, every chop bone standing up pertly in a circle, each one decorated with its elaborate paper frill. Looking at the array with fascination, Beardslee stood up to carve, asking uncertainly, "Now Frances, what do I do with this? What in the world are these paper booties?" Quietly amused at her husband's playful tone, she said, "John, just get along with the carving. We're all hungry."

Marching On

In 1969, the General Synod met in New Brunswick. It was an emotional and upsetting time. James Foreman, militant black leader, was occupying our 475 RCA offices in New York, and appeared at General Synod to demand reparations. The proposed merger with the Presbyterian Church in the U.S. had failed because of our unfavorable vote, and the denomination was facing a painful challenge for understanding and reconciliation, East and West. At the beginning of one General Synod business session, a line of Reformed Church women marched in, with banners flying, to confront the synod for the rights and needs of women as equal partners in the Reformed Church. It was an arresting sight and courageous demonstration. Midway in the line of march strode eighty-one-year-old Frances Beardslee, banner held high. She marched along with determination and resolution, impressive and awesome. Her presence was undoubtedly appreciated by her daughter-in-law, Edith Brown Beardslee, a leader of the group. To my mind and recollection, "Fearless Frances" in that march of witness, joined the pioneering women of the ages, claiming full partnership in the Christian cause. Frances lived on the New Brunswick campus in the Beardslee home on College Avenue until 1975, reaching the age of eighty-seven, her presence always a prevailing influence.

The Youngest Beardslee

One September day in 1935, we heard some faculty children on the lawn outside the open window at our Van Dyke House apartment. Playing and discussing, the natural leader of the hour was a little girl. She was later identified as Ellen Beardslee, age six, youngest child of President and Frances Beardslee. As we listened to the vocabulary of these children, it appeared to us that the members of this group were much older than they turned out to be. Little Ellen was clearly in charge of the conversation, and her discussion included words like "presume," "consideration," "speculate," "imagination," "perception," "frustration," "scientific," "consternation," and "conscious." She was clearly "one of those six going on sixteen prodigies." We soon found an answer for her remarkable, advanced vocabulary. In the context of the gifted family, of which she was the youngest member, she had exposure to language and meanings, along with the open communication style of their family life. She had an older brother, John III, at Yale; another, William Armitage, at Harvard; high-schooler Frank Palmer was bound for Cornell; grade-schooler David was later to attend Swarthmore. Ellen herself would in time attend Wellesley as her mother before her.

John W. III

In this publication, we are primarily honoring John W. Beardslee III. Some of the background we have already covered has introduced the parents and family that nurtured him. They provide the foundation for his remarkable life and ministry. As contemporaries with different educational histories, I did not really know John until the early 1960s when we began working closely together on various committees and causes for the Reformed Church in America. We joined in a common struggle for racial equality, equal rights, and empowerment of minorities as we worked together in the cause of justice and peace. My recollections are perhaps strongest of John in his work on the Christian Action Commission—where he was clearly an outstanding person on the commission. This observation should not minimize, though, his many roles and contributions. Gifted and articulate, John was also a scholar, missioner, professor, commission member, archivist, churchman, counselor, social activist, ecumenist, devotional leader, historian, theologian, and friend.

Like Father, Like Son

John was truly a reflection of his father before him. He demonstrated this particularly as a careful scholar and effective teacher. Vernon H. Kooy, in the *New Brunswick Theological Seminary Newsletter* of March 1984, describes John as a teacher:

> He has the unique ability to see to the heart of issues and to make cautious and sober judgments upon them. Rumor has it that his lectures, given without notes, were like reading a book. He would stop precisely at the close of the hour, even in the middle of a sentence. At the next session he would begin exactly where he left off, finish the sentence and continue lecturing. He will long and fondly be remembered as a scholar, teacher and friend.

Going to Court

I recall the occasion when John and I went to court in Trenton, New Jersey, to be available as witnesses for young Glen Pontier, who was on trial for refusal to participate in military service.

John (as a member of various commissions and committees for the church) was prepared to review the Christian church's stand on members who refused to engage in war, and I was to explain the statements and positions of the Reformed Church in America (as general secretary) and of the World Alliance of Reformed Churches on conscientious objection and civil disobedience.

It was a sobering letdown for us, after considerable consultation and preparation together, to have our proposed testimonies declared inadmissible by the judge, on the grounds that the only legal point at issue was obedience or disobedience to the draft law.

However, I was greatly impressed with John Beardslee's genuine concern for the rights of conscience and the well-being of a son of the Reformed Church in America. "After all," said John, "most of what informs and binds Glen's conscience was taught to him and learned in the manse, church schools, worship services, and educational institutions of the Reformed Church in America." Involved in the protest statements and marches of the 1960s, Beardslee encouraged his students to take responsible stands and make a courageous witness to society on current social issues.

Christian Action

John was a member of the Christian Action Commission of the Reformed Church in America from 1960 to 1966. Here he headed various subcommittees and helped prepare statements on many social issues for General Synod's consideration. He was a tower of strength, dependable, well balanced, respectful of differing positions, historically conscious, and always patient and relentless in his fight for justice.

Some of the subjects studied and reported on from 1960 to 1966 were: Human Rights and Race Relations, International Relations and Conflicts, How to Combat Communism, Premises Regarding Communism, Theological Basis for Christian Action, Human Rights and Civil Rights, Fair Housing, Empowerment of Women, Right of Dissent and Conscientious Objection, Concern for the Poor, Church and Economic Life, Divorce and Remarriage, Prayer in Public Schools, Christian Citizenship, Capital Punishment, and Statements on South Africa, Red China, Vietnam, Liquor Traffic, and Gambling. To all these areas, John Beardslee applied his insights, balanced judgment, resourceful mind, and strong convictions.

It is good to know that Beardslee's voice is still being heard, strong and appreciated. The November 1, 1985, issue of *Hotline* reported that:

A continuing education event "Hope in the Midst of Despair" will be held November 4 and 5, 1985, at the Warwick Conference Center. Main speaker is John W. Beardslee III, who will look at the church as a historical and present resistance movement.

South Africa Struggles

I was also associated with John for many years (1967 to 1977) in our discussion and conferences with the Reformed churches in South Africa. We served together on the Ad Hoc Committee on South Africa, continuing from 1969 to 1976, striving for open discussions, understanding, mutual support, and unity.

In 1970, at the World Alliance of Reformed Churches Twentieth General Council in Nairobi, Kenya, discussions were held between our Reformed Church delegates and the South Africa Reformed delegates. The only substantial result was an agreement to discuss several concerns having to do with social and economic justice and equality in the light of the biblical record with representatives from the white, black, colored, and Indian Reformed churches.

The meeting itself, however, was an unhappy one. Presided over as usual by the head of the mother church delegation, it began in friendliness but soon became very emotional as the two colored representatives expressed their feelings of frustration and irritation about their actual relationships in the South Africa situation. When this occurred, the presider abruptly adjourned the meeting. A group photograph which had been arranged was taken, but one of the delegates, Wilbur Washington, respectfully declined to join in the picture.

For several years we continued correspondence in persistent hope, and seized every opportunity for fraternal exchanges with representatives of all four of the Reformed churches in South Africa.

In spite of every effort, we were unable to complete an agenda of topics for consideration (as agreed to at Nairobi) because of frustrating delays and the insistence of the mother church to control the agenda and its unwillingness to accept the other Reformed church representatives as equal participants.

In 1972, we succeeded in opening up direct correspondence and exchanging delegates with the daughter churches (black, colored, and Indian) in South Africa, much to the displeasure of the mother church (white).

Ten years later, in 1982, the General Synod of the Reformed Church in America voted "to suspend further dialogue until such a time as the NGK (mother) church renounces apartheid and enters into conversations on an equal basis with the other Reformed Churches in South Africa" (Minutes of General Synod, 1982, p. 139).

In spite of years of effort and persistent negotiations, it seemed to us that the mountain labored mightily and brought forth a disappointing mouse.

Archivist

As a church historian, John W. Beardslee III instinctively knew that we should look back on our past with appreciation and discernment, so that we can more clearly see the way before us.

John served as archivist for the Reformed Church in America from 1967 to 1978. Since the denominational archives were housed in the "Dutch Church Room" of Gardner Sage Library at New Brunswick Theological Seminary, his service as archivist was a natural one. With two part-time assistants, Elsie B. Stryker and Emma Roberts, along with student wives as helpers, John supervised the archival program for over a decade.

As stated clerk I was associated with the Advisory Committee on History (1960), which evolved into the Permanent Committee on History (1963), and which was reorganized into the Permanent Commission on History in 1966. As archivist, John was responsible for the denominational archives, to classify, preserve, and maintain the records and documents for present and future generations.

The record of accomplishments of our work with the Commission on History included:

1. Archival programs (expanded) at Hope, Central, and Northwestern colleges, in addition to New Brunswick

2. Microfilming and camera equipment, and reader, for recording and research

3. "Historical Series of the Reformed Church in America" (13 volumes published from 1969 to 1986), to make known the history and heritage of the church

4. Collection of records from General Synod, particular synods, classes, local churches, program boards, commissions and committees, and institutions

5. *Historical Directory of the Reformed Church in America, 1628 to 1978* (revised edition), with historical data on all Reformed Church in America ministers and churches

6. *Digest and Index of the Minutes of the General Synod* (first edition, 1958-1977; second edition, 1906-1957, published 1978 and 1982, respectively), referencing all important actions of the General Synod.

By 1977, the work of the Commission on History and the development of the archival program was so well established and appreciated that the General Synod approved an expanded program, and appointed the first permanent archivist, Mr. Russell Gasero. John W. Beardslee III's historical sense and intuition provided focus for this expansion. He promoted collecting and preserving the important records, facilitating scholarly research, publishing historical data, and encouraging a greater historical sensitivity to the times in which we live.

All of this seems a providential prelude to the present search for the meaning and importance of our denominational identity as "A People Who Belong." By his determined work to keep our history alive and useful, John has made, and continues to make, a unique and substantial impact on our Reformed Church.

The Beardslees as Teachers

The teaching and ministry of the three Beardslee generations in the Reformed Church in America spans from 1864 to the present. It is an outstanding record of service. The Beardslee ministry represents collectively 155 years (to 1986), of which 123 years were in the classroom.

John W. Beardslee, Sr., was born in Sandusky, Ohio. Trained at Rutgers University and New Brunswick Theological Seminary, he was a pastor in Constantine, Michigan (1864-84), and in Troy, New York (1884-88), for twenty-four years. His teaching career extended thirty-three years—as professor at Western Theological Seminary (1888-1917), and as lector at New Brunswick Seminary (1917-21). In 1913 the library and its building at Western Seminary was named "Beardslee Memorial Library" on the occasion of his twenty-fifth year as professor. He died at age eighty-four in 1921.

John W. Beardslee, Jr., was educated at Hope College, Western Seminary, and the University of Chicago (M.A. and Ph.D.). His teaching career included Hope College (1905-13), Western Seminary (1913-17), and New Brunswick Seminary (1917-49), a total of forty-four years. After retirement at seventy, he continued as part-time teacher and acting dean until 1955, completing fifty years. He died in 1962, at age eighty-two.

John W. Beardslee III was educated at Yale University (A.B. 1935 and Ph.D. 1957) and Princeton Theological Seminary (1941). His teaching included Basrah, Iraq (1935-38), Annville Institute (1943-44), George Washington University (1948-51), Central College (1951-64), and New Brunswick Seminary (1964-84). A pastor for two years (First Reformed Church, Tarrytown, New York), John's teaching covered over forty years. He continues to assist New Brunswick Seminary in Gardner Sage Library and in other capacities.

And it seems the tradition continues. The Beardslee era now has a fourth generation Beardslee, Nancy Eunice, daughter of John III and Edith, who continues in ministry. With an M.Div. from Perkins Divinity School and as a member of the Texas Conference of the United Methodist Church, Nancy is presently a student at New Brunswick Theological Seminary in preparation for specialized ministry.

In Appreciation

Nothing can so poignantly evoke the flavor of the receding past as some remembered tune, some melody that has caught up and woven into its own unconscious fabric the very color and fragrance of a day gone by.

Alexander Woolcott

Woolcott's words describe well the special experience I have had putting together these memories of the Beardslee family. My appreciation, especially for John W. Beardslee, Jr., as my professor in New Testament and for John W. Beardslee III as my contemporary and fellow worker, was again stirred up. I found myself thinking about the large place memory has in our life and education.

I realized anew how much my life, as well as the lives of countless others, has been enlarged and enriched through association with the Beardslees, who have worked long, wisely, and well, both through their words and by example. These memories— representing what is strong, and good—may well provide the "best education."

And so, to all the Beardslees, we thank you—not only for the important memories you have created but also for the lasting influence you have on our lives.

II
Advocacy for Social Justice in the Reformed Church in America

Arie R. Brouwer

Historian, archivist, ecumenist, and advocate for social justice are all roles in which John W. Beardslee III will be found in the front ranks of those who have served the Reformed Church in America. Others will discuss his specific contributions. I wish merely to note my appreciation for the perspectives and persistence which Professor Beardslee applied to each of these areas. During the time I served the Reformed Church in America as a denominational executive, and particularly while serving as general secretary, I turned to him again and again for authoritative information on historical resources and informed reflection on the life of the church. He was always helpful.

Nor have his contributions been limited to the Reformed Church in America. He has been an active ecumenist bearing a strong witness to the unity of the church through private and public correspondence, preaching and teaching, and regular wise counsel offered to the General Synod which he frequently served as a delegate. He has also contributed significantly to the ecumenical movement through participation in a variety of conferences, meetings, and publications.

But it is of social concern that I have been asked to write. I am pleased to do so, for that is the role through which Professor Beardslee has most often inspired and encouraged me. The name of Beardslee has for me always been surrounded by an aura of history and learning, since I knew it first in connection with the library at Western Seminary named in honor of another Professor Beardslee, this professor's father. Given those associations of learning and history, and knowing something of the distinguished Beardslee family tradition, I listened with special interest when I first heard Professor Beardslee speak. His was a vigorous statement of advocacy for social justice delivered at a General Synod meeting. In the General Synod meetings since (a total of twenty) I have heard him speak again and again as an advocate for social justice. Sometimes he spoke almost alone, because his longer vision reached beyond the horizon accepted by the body as a whole. More often he spoke with profound insight and startling clarity about issues which many others saw—but less well.

Little wonder then that I always welcomed the sight of John Beardslee approaching a microphone at General Synod. He invariably enriched the discussion. Taken as a whole, his speeches were statements of conviction and abandon, combining a rare mixture of passion in speech, depth in learning, clarity in thought, and eloquence in language which honored and served us all.

This tribute may strike some of my readers as one advocate for social justice honoring another of like mind. My appreciation is undeniably enhanced by the fact that the quality of John Beardslee's witness has helped to stimulate and sustain my own. But that appreciation is rooted more deeply in another fact—namely, that the quality of character and speech which I here celebrate is compellingly visible even when one may differ vigorously. During the fifteen years in which I served as a denominational executive (1968-83), John and I have argued and augmented one another's witness in committee and commission meetings as well as through private and public correspondence and conversation. I treasure the memory of those encounters and feel my life and witness strengthened and enriched by them.

But these few lines of public appreciation will no doubt already have outstripped my friend's capacity to conceal his embarrassment. He will be impatient that I have not yet begun to write of the issues concerning advocacy for social justice in the Reformed Church in America. Since I write to honor his witness, I accede to what I suppose to be his wish, beginning with a brief historical review—a methodology which I suppose the professor would approve, even though we will no doubt have another round of correspondence about what follows!

My intention, however, is not to discuss, or even to sketch, the history of advocacy for social justice in the Reformed Church in America. I wish only to identify some of the historical themes and characteristics of that advocacy as a background for looking at the present challenge. If for some I leave too much historical space between the lines, to them I commend the chapter on "Social Concerns" by Jerome De Jong in *Piety and Patriotism*.[1]

Calvinist and Evangelical

We in the Reformed Church in America—both East and West— are Calvinists and evangelicals. To be sure, some of us are more Calvinist and some of us more evangelical, and there are a few other convictions around the edges. But taken as a whole, in a single phrase, we are, I think, best described as evangelical Calvinists.

The Calvinism, I suppose, needs no defense and little explanation. Our grandfathers and grandmothers—or at least our great-great-grandfathers and mothers—were Calvinist to the core. Given the mixture of commercial interest in Nieuw Amsterdam and later the mixed motivations of evangelical religion in "new" Holland, Zeeland, Overisel, and Drenthe as well as in Pella and Orange City, the New World communities never embodied Calvinism in quite the same way that some had in the Netherlands. But a good part of the core of our community was and still is solidly in the tradition of John Calvin.

The evangelicalism is also of long standing. Stimulated in the East by the Great Awakening of the eighteenth century, which for the Reformed Church in America was focused particularly in the ministry of Theodorus J. Frelinghuysen on the frontier in New Jersey, it eventually triumphed over the traditional Calvinism of New York and other settled communities. In the West, evangelicalism was at the root of the struggle which had led to schism in the Netherlands and was therefore the raison d'être of "the community" at Holland and of the refuge at Pella.

Both of these currents, Calvinist and evangelical, carried the Reformed Church toward involvement in the social life of the new nation. The Calvinist concern for personal and social transformation merged with the evangelical concern for individual conversion to produce a torrent of rhetoric about making America "a truly Christian country" which would be "a teacher of nations" and "a city set upon a hill." The vision was essentially Calvinist, but the methodology (and zeal) was evangelical. The Calvinism of the Old World had relied heavily on the traditional link with the state whose Christian laws and magistrates would both restrain evil and secure the ministry of the church for righteousness. The separation of church and state following the War for Independence invalidated that appeal—at least officially. The amazing success of the Great Awakening early in the eighteenth century led quite naturally to a reliance on the evangelical approach to social transformation, that is, the conversion of individuals who would then together provide the foundation for social good. In his introduction to the Constitution of the Reformed Church in America, published in 1792, John Henry Livingston hailed the separation of church and state and the opportunity for evangelical voluntarism with patriotic and religious zeal:

> Whatever relates to the immediate authority and interposition of the Magistrate in the government of the Church, and which is introduced more or less into all the national establishments in Europe, is entirely omitted in the Constitution now published. Whether the Church of Christ will not be more effectually patronized in a civil government where full freedom of conscience and worship is equally protected and insured to all men, and where truth is left to vindicate her own sovereign authority and influence, than where men in power promote their favorite denominations by temporal emoluments and partial discriminations, will now, in America, have a fair trial; and all who know and love the truth will rejoice in the prospect which such a happy situation affords for the triumph of the Gospel, and the reign of peace and love.[2]

But the Calvinist vision and evangelical methodology did not always work together smoothly. Frequently, there was conflict and confusion. This is readily apparent in the handling of the two social causes which were most prominent in the Calvinist and evangelical denominations in America during the eighteenth and nineteenth centuries and well into the twentieth: Sabbath observance and temperance. Sabbath observance was a hallmark of the Calvinist heritage of church-state relations in Europe. Calvinists in eighteenth- and nineteenth-century America buttressed the old arguments for a Christian society by adducing the social benefits which flowed from societal observance of the Sabbath, especially as a means of controlling the greed of corporations and ensuring a day of rest and family nurture for workers. Identification with the American way of church-state separation however precluded the old Calvinistic methodology of Sabbath legislation. It pointed instead toward reliance on the evangelical methodology of preaching and persuasion. When that methodology proved unequal to the task, the advocates of Sabbath observance fell back on the arguments from social benefits and contended that observance of Sunday rest was in fact a civic institution which could be defended on that ground alone and therefore should be a part of the common law. Although many such laws were successfully enacted, they eventually also gave way before the forces of secularization. As they fell, only a relatively few voices could be heard protesting lost social good. Most—and surely the loudest—voices denounced it as (another) sign of national godlessness.

Temperance (American style with a capital T) was another *cause célèbre* in nineteenth- and twentieth-century America. Calvin and his followers had of course a good deal to say about temperance (lowercase t), moderation, and self-discipline, but the prohibition of alcoholic beverages had no more place in Calvin than in Paul. The old Calvinism in the Reformed Church in America (represented particularly by recent Dutch immigrants) indeed expressed considerable reservation about such anti-alcoholic stringency, publicly expressing concern over the possible exclusion of wine at the Lord's Supper—and no doubt harboring a few other private reservations! Those reservations notwithstanding, the General Synod of 1914 appointed a committee on temperance and went on record in favor of prohibition.

Evangelical Legalism

A new style of political action had now come to full flower. The traditional Calvinist church-state relationship had been put aside as an Old World phenomenon. But the early confidence in the power of evangelical preaching and persuasion had also declined. In the place of both had come a form of evangelical legalism which sought to coerce compliance with evangelical values by means of public pressure or legislation rather than relying on the voluntary agreement which constitutes the very heart of evangelical Christianity.

Ironically, the triumph of evangelical legalism marked by Prohibition was also the beginning of its temporary eclipse. The devastation of World War I, burgeoning affluence, rapid urbanization, and increasing secularization all contributed to the erosion of evangelical influence during the 1920s. The savage treatment of William Jennings Bryan, the recognized leader of evangelicals, at the hands of the press during the Scopes trial and Bryan's death shortly after in 1925, as well as the repeal of Prohibition in the early 1930s drove the evangelicals deeper and deeper into personal and private religion. Only recently has that influence reemerged in a burst of resurgent evangelical legalism.

I have already suggested that, although evangelical legalism may draw on both the Reformed and evangelical traditions, it is faithful to neither and in conflict with both. The controversies over prayer in the public schools and Sabbath observance may illustrate the differences.

If my description of the Reformed Church in America as a community of evangelical Calvinists is accurate, then we may assume that we (particularly as Calvinists) have a common concern for the spiritual foundations of our society. Further, the record shows that we have long since reformed our traditional Calvinist doctrine of church and state to make way for their separation in the cultural and religious pluralism which defines modern American society. As Reformed evangelicals in America we therefore eschew legislation which would coerce compliance with our confession of faith. We rely instead on the preaching of the Word, the witness of the church, and the ministry of the Spirit. Our confession is, in other words, a matter of faith rather than of law. We would, therefore, oppose any attempt to prohibit voluntary prayer as strongly as we would also oppose any attempt by the state to prescribe prayers. Neither prohibition nor prescription are the business of the state.

Similarly our concern for the social value of rest from daily work requires something other than arguments for the social value of Sabbath observance. Rather, it requires arguments which would place no special emphasis on the particular day, which would, in other words, be completely disinterested. That is, it would have no special benefit for us or for those who share our religious view. Such legislation would rather seek to ensure equal rights. Legislation for a forty-hour week with full freedom for those whose days of rest and/or worship are other than our own would therefore be one way to enshrine the spirit of the Sabbath in the law of the land— protecting all while coercing the conscience of none.

Faithfulness to our own values will, in fact, sometimes require us to seek legislation which erodes our own privileges in order to secure the rights of others, for example, in the area of racial justice. Indeed, it is this vision of serving the common good with special concern for the rights of the oppressed even if at the expense of one's own privileges while coercing the conscience of none which distinguishes authentic Christian social witness from self-serving legalism. Not secure in confessing faith, evangelical legalism seeks to coerce piety. It claims privilege instead of prophesying justice. It is therefore to be sharply distinguished from the earlier evangelical, and frequently Reformed, social witness which led to the abolition of slavery, women's suffrage, and prison reform. These and others were triumphs of social justice which served the common good, totally unlike the partisan privilege championed by evangelical legalism, which defines the common good in terms of its own piety and preferences and seeks to compel compliance.

Cultural Conservatism

Evangelical legalism is often closely allied with cultural conservatism. Jerome De Jong has shown how cultural conservatism led the Reformed Church generally to oppose both the pro-slavery and abolitionist forces prior to the Civil War without significant direct involvement in the struggle against slavery itself. The widely accepted evangelical methodology of individual conversion aided and abetted this unhappy evenhandedness by being content with preaching against the slavery of sin in the heart of slave and slave-owner alike.

Cultural conservatism is by no means unique to the Reformed Church in America. It pervades American Protestantism and seems to dominate American fundamentalism where the Bible seems sometimes scarcely visible through the folds of the flag and where God seems more to serve the nation than vice versa. It may be argued, in fact, that our lingering Old World ethnic identity has saved us from some of the snares of confusing the way of Christ with the American way. But then it may also be argued that our awareness of being perceived as Dutch and different has made us more eager to conform. Both positions are no doubt partly correct.

A more important source of cultural conservatism is surely the solid middle-class character of the membership of the Reformed Church in America. America, at least until recently, has been the land of middle-class privilege and plenty. Since more than a few of us are the children or grandchildren of poor immigrants, we have special reasons for gratitude. Saluting the flag comes naturally. Protesting against policy does not. To many, it seems in fact disloyal.

But protesting against the powers may also be understood as a call to a deeper loyalty—and even as a call to conserve. It is not, to be sure, a call to conserve a particular cultural experience. It is concerned rather with the enduring values of truth, peace, justice, freedom, faith, hope, and love which have been forged in the crucible of human experience since the beginning of time. As Christians, we are governed particularly by the shape and content of those values set forth in Scripture and developed in the tradition of the church. And it is these values, these standards of faith and life, which we are particularly charged to uphold and which by their enduring worth and transcendent quality can set us free from the cultural conservatism of a particular time and place.

We might say then that what we need are conservatives with a longer and broader memory—conservatives who govern their lives not by the experiences and values of a particular time and place, but who live as much as possible in the light of God's whole work in history. The risk of saying it that way is that God's call is not to conserve the past but to join with all the ages in the continuing work of renewal, looking toward the new heaven and the new earth which the Spirit is bringing into being. Even the longest and broadest memory possible is no substitute for that vision, but it may help to keep us open to that vision by protecting us from the short and narrow memory which makes us the prisoners of cultural conservatism.

Civil Order

Cultural conservatism takes many forms. One particularly powerful form of long standing is of special importance, namely, concern for the civil order. The Reformed tradition, along with most other traditions in the Christian church, has historically placed great emphasis on maintaining the civil order—and rightly so. Maintenance of the civil order is a fundamental need for the well-being of society. Government must be taken seriously and disobeyed only in situations when all reasonable hope for resolution of severe grievances through established processes has been exhausted.

A number of factors in the contemporary world make such situations increasingly common: the accelerating militarization of governments and their accompanying obsession with secrecy; the consequent collapse of political processes leading to widespread disinterest, despair, and cynicism; and the worldwide denial of human rights with imprisonment, torture, disappearance, and extrajudicial executions becoming commonplace in many societies. All these have led many people who seek change to see no recourse other than civil disobedience. Many are our sisters and brothers in Christ who believe they are compelled to disobey the authorities in order to be obedient to Christ. Some live in other lands; some live in our own land. For some, disobedience is a matter of life and death: for others it is a matter of tax resistance, of public protest, of imprisonment or some other form of lesser suffering. Their growing call for support and their complaint that our compliance with the powers is increasing their suffering more and more compels us all to face the questions of our own obedience and disobedience.

The prospect of fruitful discussion is, of course, greatly complicated and highly charged emotionally by the revolutionary romanticism and even anarchism that is popularly associated— sometimes rightly, sometimes wrongly—with civil disobedience. But point is well made in the May 1983 issue of *Sojourners* which is a solid and sober attempt to reopen the discussion

The framework for our discussion is, of course, that of the Scriptures and the Christian tradition, with particular reference to the Reformed tradition. Our use of Scripture must go beyond our traditionally heavy emphasis on Romans 13 with its admonition that "every person be subject to the governing authorities." We must, for example, pay attention as well to Revelation 13 which paints a picture of the state having set itself against God and having become an instrument of disorder rather than order. This is precisely what many Christians in many countries are claiming is happening again today. But these two chapters (which both happen to be numbered 13) are only a beginning. The situation today compels us to listen carefully to all that the New Testament has to say about the relationship of Christians to the civil order and to pray for wisdom to discern our own.

A reexamination of our tradition may also be rewarding. Most of us seem to have overlooked Calvin's qualified provision for revolt against a higher magistrate which he said could be legitimate if led by a lower magistrate. We have not adequately recognized that teaching as a revolutionary departure from the medieval absolutism which prevailed before the Reformation. And we have emphatically not taken it as a step along the way for the church always reforming and, therefore, as a basis for continuing examination of the prerogatives of the civil authority. A. J. Muste, whom we honor in the annual Muste Award presented by New Brunswick Seminary, of which John Beardslee was a 1984 recipient, once observed that

"Holy Disobedience" could become "a virtue, indeed a necessary and indispensable measure of spiritual self-preservation."[3] Many today would echo that argument; we all need to weigh it.

Advocacy for Social Justice in America

We are challenged today by those Christians in many lands who plead with the world Christian community to support them in their struggles against the principalities and powers. We know a few of these sisters and brothers by name. Many more are unknown to us. But however many they are, they are few compared to the vast numbers who live in various stages of despair and hopelessness. They are in despair because the foundations of world peace and social order are crumbling. More arms, more poverty, more hunger, more crime, more locked doors, more fear—the evidence is inescapable. We respond in a variety of ways. We may try to pretend that it is not so. We may try to hold the foundations together. We may hope that somebody will be able to do something. We may try to build walls to protect our own interests. We may give up in despair or cynicism, or we may join the spoilers. Our dilemma is, in other words, not merely a matter of civil order but of the life of the world.

For this life of the world, the churches in the United States bear a special responsibility. This is so by virtue of the special role of the United States in the world. One may, and I think must, readily acknowledge that the United States by no means dominates the world today as it did forty, thirty, twenty, or even ten years ago. And one may readily acknowledge that the Soviet Union has indeed grown vastly more powerful over that same period—to say nothing of the People's Republic of China. Nevertheless, it is indisputable that the United States is still, and barring catastrophe will likely remain for some time to come, by far the most powerful nation in the world. It leads its chief rival culturally, economically, scientifically, technologically, politically, and militarily. It is, of course, not single-handedly responsible for all the ills of the world. Nor can it alone cause justice to prevail. But it can do more to bring justice about than any other single nation. And that makes the witness of the churches for justice in the United States of paramount importance, not only to our own people but to all the people of the world.

Happily, our churches are equipped with a great many resources to support this witness. Many have suffered decline, to be sure, but they are still strong—numerically, economically, and institutionally. Further, the mainline churches in the United States are among those in the world most committed to ecumenical action for peace and justice. Most of the major denominations maintain offices in Washington and are active in the National Council of Churches and other forums of ecumenical action.

The social and legal traditions of the United States also provide the churches with the freedom to act. The government does place certain restrictions on the activities of the churches and has occasionally interfered in their ministries. But they are among the freest in the world and both the courts and forums of public opinion undergird their freedom to witness and act. Moreover, the moral tradition of the nation—at least some prominent strains in that tradition—has itself been largely shaped by the values of the Western Christian tradition and thus provides a broad basis for Christian witness for peace and justice.

And, finally, the pluralism of the society, encompassing as it does representatives of most of the world's peoples and religions, provides an opportunity for Christians in the United States to experience directly the conflicts and controversies surrounding many of the issues of peace and justice, whereas Christians in other lands can know many of them only secondhand. Such firsthand experience almost automatically provides resources for leadership.

Nurturing Advocacy

From the beginning, the Reformed Church in America has been reckoned among the mainline churches in the United States. It continues to share in responsibility for nurturing an advocacy for social justice which can in turn sustain and nurture the life of the world.

Our first responsibility is, I think, theological. We ourselves may bemoan our lack of formal theological discussion and publication and compare ourselves unfavorably to some other denominations. Yet there is another side to the story—a kind of theological steadiness that keeps us on course, a deep current that guides our general direction. Most of the churches with whom we have worked regularly in the ecumenical movement recognize that in us, sometimes better than we do ourselves. We should tap that strength.

The situation of our world teetering on the verge of despair and hopelessness cries out for clear and forceful statements of faith which are fully engaged with the crucial issues of our time. We need, in other words, to do some fresh theological work on the old biblical and Reformed doctrine of the sovereignty of God. We need to show the present meaning of the ancient prophetic passion for justice and their centuries-old affirmation of faith that justice will prevail. We need to let it be known that God's righteousness will reign. And we need to show that in Christ God is already present in the world working toward the fulfillment of all creation. Our songs and sermons and services of worship must make the message plain.

Our second responsibility is to follow the prophets in personally involving ourselves in the struggle. Direct involvement gives credibility; it calls people from hopelessness and despair to hope and courage as nothing else can. This was surely true of the prophets themselves who witnessed against false kings at risk of life itself. It was no less true of the father of our Reformed tradition whose deep involvement in advocacy for social justice in Geneva both underscored and refined his teaching, giving it a quality which has shaped the centuries.

The example of such community leaders reminds us that the burden of involvement falls especially on leadership whether local, regional, or national. Their example is a powerful force, inspiring rising generations of advocates for social justice as well as motivating people to take up the present challenge. Such involvement is very often costly and may involve suffering. But there is strength for that in the suffering of Christ whose self-emptying in life and death is the source of our strength for our witness and work in the world.

Our third responsibility is to provide firsthand experience with people who suffer from war and injustice. Knowledge of the systems which cause oppression is, of course, essential. But there is nothing like personal experience to make that knowledge live, or to lead one to seek more knowledge, or to believe what one already knows but has so far been unable to believe. For commitment to racial justice, economic justice, justice for women, or any kind of justice, there is no substitute for firsthand experience with the victims of injustice.

But this is not so easy as it sounds. Victims of injustice are often in a dependent posture of some sort, frequently because they receive funds. Authentic relationships are very difficult, if not impossible, under those circumstances. Every effort must therefore be made first to secure for the victims of injustice an assurance of an equal place to stand—before they are asked to enter into dialogue. Although this may be a painful and difficult process, it is an essential prerequisite for building relationships with integrity.

Conclusion

Nurturing advocates for social justice is of course not a new thing for the Reformed Church in America. I have myself experienced it in this community and count it as one of the greatest debts I owe the church. The turning point for me was surely the ministry in the Bethel Reformed Church in Passaic, New Jersey, which brought me into direct contact with issues of racial and ethnic oppression I had not earlier known. A little over a year after moving to Passaic, I was elected to the Board of World Mission which led to another wholly new set of experiences and to the discovery that the oppression experienced by the poor on a daily basis in Passaic was essentially very similar to that faced by urban poor around the world.

Both within and beyond the Reformed Church in America it has been my privilege to know personally many people from all over the world who have invested their whole beings in the struggle for social justice. Knowing them is of course an inspiration. But it is also a frustration. I think that I shall never forget the feeling of helplessness and rage when we who were gathered in the Reformed Church's Ecumenical Consultation in 1980 heard the news of the arrest and imprisonment of Dr. C. M. Kao, general secretary of the Presbyterian Church in Taiwan. Our feelings were the more intense because we had been talking about building worldwide networks of ecumenical solidarity, and because the presence at the consultation of one of Dr. Kao's friends personalized the pain for us. To be sure, Dr. Kao has just been released as I write, but only after more than four years of imprisonment. In many other cases, there are no releases and sometimes not even any news.

And that is why advocacy for peace and justice is first and last a matter of faith—"the assurance of things hoped for, the conviction of things not seen" (Hebrews 11:1). Only by faith can one continue to seek the new Jerusalem while the cities we know die around us. Only by faith can one continue to seek the new heaven and the new earth while air and sea and land are polluted. Only by faith can one seek the peaceable kingdom while the whole creation groans under the burden of arms.

The life of John W. Beardslee III testifies to such faith.

III
Reformed Perspectives on War and Peace

John Hubers

The horrifying prospect of a major confrontation which would unleash the destructive arsenals of the United States and Russia has forced Christians from many different traditions to reassess their thinking about war. Recent studies and proposals made by our own General Synod, such as the 1981 resolution urging Reformed Church in America congregations "to engage in a serious study of the meaning of Christian peacemaking in today's world,"[1] reflect this growing concern.

Such rethinking cannot, however, be done in a vacuum. The desire to wrestle with this issue today requires a willingness to confront our past honestly and humbly. Reformed Church in America statements which condemn the use of violence in modern revolutionary movements, for instance, will have little or no impact unless we are willing to come to grips with our own violent revolutionary roots. Before we proceed in new directions on the issue of Christian participation in war it is important that we recognize the forces which have shaped present opinions.

This paper attempts to speak to this need by bringing together for the purpose of analysis, position papers and pronouncements on the topics of war and peace formulated by General Synod during crisis points in American history. In particular, the areas of interest are the Revolutionary War, the Civil War, the Spanish-American War, World War I, World War II, and the Vietnam War. Other wars, such as the War of 1812 or the Korean War, do not appear to have merited special consideration by synod, or they too would have been included.

In doing a study of this nature certain shortcomings must be recognized. First, synod is a representative body in the loose sense of the word. A majority vote on a resolution does not necessarily give an accurate picture of the body it represents. Secondly, dealing only with final resolutions or position papers does not enable us to see behind the scenes at the soul-searching and often bitter debates such statements evoked. This side of the picture needs to be fleshed out by other studies. On the other hand, it must be said that the General Synod represents the highest court of appeal for the Reformed Church opinion as a denomination, and that the statements under consideration here were presented as official Reformed Church in America policy. It is in this manner that they will be evaluated—as "official statements" of the denomination made in times of national crisis, at those points in American history when our ecclesiastical soul was most exposed to the gaze of a world in search of ethical direction.

Christians and War

The Three Basic Viewpoints

Roland Bainton, in his book *Christian Attitudes Toward War and Peace*, notes that Christians have formulated at least three different approaches to war:

> Broadly speaking, three attitudes to war and peace were to appear in the Christian ethic: pacifism, the just war, and the crusade. Chronologically they emerged in just this order. The early church was pacifist to the time of Constantine. Then, partly as a result of the close association of emperor and partly by reason of the threat of barbarian invasions, Christians in the fourth and fifth centuries took over from the classical world the doctrine of the just war, whose object should be to vindicate justice and restore peace. The crusade arose in the high Middle Ages, a holy war fought under the auspices of the church or of some inspired religious leader, not on behalf of justice conceived in terms of life and property, but on behalf of an ideal, the Christian faith.[2]

These, of course, are not categories set in concrete, but represent trends of thought which have predominated during certain periods of church history. What is important to realize is that all three have been considered as options from the Christian point of view, and, in fact, have continued in one form or another as components of Christian thought up to the present day. In addition, it must be noted that these categories can be broken down into numerous subgroupings, so that each represents a wide spectrum of opinion. John Yoder, for instance, identifies at least seventeen different forms of pacifism, a list which surprisingly contains the just war theory, an attitude which he labels, "the pacifism of the honest of cases."[3] Yet despite such fluidity, these basic approaches serve as useful tools by which to analyze Christian attitudes toward war, and will be used as such in this essay.

Before proceeding with the task at hand, it is important that we take a closer look at the two positions which have been most predominant in Reformed circles, namely, the just war and holy war concepts. A fundamental understanding of both is needed to help explain certain attitudes which are found in synod pronouncements.

The Just War

It was Augustine who gave classic shape to the just war approach to conflict between nations. The first three centuries of Christianity had been marked by a pacifism which viewed participation in warfare as contrary to the spirit of Christ. Lactantius, writing as late as A.D. 304-305, summed up the teaching of the leading theologians of both East and West when he wrote,

> God in prohibiting killing discountenances not only brigandage, which is contrary to human laws, but also that which men regard as legal. Participation in warfare, therefore, will not be legitimate to a just man whose military service is justice.[4]

This was the position of a minority group within a largely pagan society. Upon the conversion of Constantine, however, a radical change took place in terms of the Christian understanding of government. The problem now became how to justify what appeared to be a necessary function of the Christian state, especially in the face of a growing threat from the fringe of the empire. It was this new situation which prompted Augustine's reappraisal of the Christian's response to war.

It should be noted at the outset that the foundation for the just war position was laid by the pacifism of the first three centuries. Augustine was not challenging the basic assumption which lay behind the pacifistic position—that the Christian should be a peacemaker whose life is a witness to sacrificial love. This is one reason why Yoder can classify it as a nonviolent alternative. War is viewed as a last resort which is only justifiable under extreme circumstances, an emphasis which if taken seriously should severely curtail Christian participation in armed conflict. As Yoder says:

> Such a position does not grant that war is always right, which would be to sell out morally to whatever government wants to do. Nor does this position believe that it is possible for the church to call upon the state to help her in her theological concerns with a holy war or crusade. To be honest we can at most say, according to this line of thought, that war might sometimes be justifiable.[5]

It is this reluctance to wage war which provides the backdrop for what Bainton calls Augustine's "Code of War." By this he means the qualifications which Augustine saw as being necessarily present for a given war to be labeled "just." They are as follows:[6]

1) The end pursued in a just war must be the restoration of peace. This means that war fought purely on the basis of national self-interest or territorial aggrandizement was not justified. The end sought must be in keeping with the Christian imperative of peace and sacrificial love.

2) Closely linked to this first requirement was that of the vindication of justice as the object of the just war. In the words of Augustine himself: "those wars may be defined as just which avenge injuries." Bainton notes that Augustine was vague as to what constituted an injury serious enough to warrant a call to arms (a vagueness which is often found in modern applications of this viewpoint as well). Despite this weakness, however, the intent of the first two qualifications was to define just wars as those fought in self-defense or to right injustices.

3) The just war must be fought in the spirit of Christian love. Those who have looked at an enemy through the sight of a gun may well wonder how it is possible to squeeze the trigger in a spirit of

Christian love, but to Augustine this was not only possible, but a requirement of just war. In his own words:

> If it is supposed that God could not enjoin warfare because in after times it was said by the Lord Jesus Christ; "I say to you, Resist not evil. . . ," the answer is that what is here required is not a bodily action but an inward disposition. . . Moses in putting to death sinners was moved not by cruelty but by love. So also was Paul when he committed the offender to Satan for the destruction of his flesh. Love does not preclude a benevolent severity nor the correction which compassion itself dictates.[7]

4) The just war may only be waged under the authority of an officially recognized government. It is the ruler, and the ruler alone, who can determine if the sword is to be used in a conflict. This may help to explain why Luther, who was a sixteenth-century advocate of the just war position, so violently opposed the peasant rebellion in Germany—citizens had no right to take the law into their own hands, no matter how unjust their situation might be. This may also explain the discrepancy in the thought of modern-day advocates of this position who justify war waged by governments but oppose violent revolutionary movements.

5) The just war must be conducted according to humane rules (as humane as may be expected during time of war). In Augustine's day this meant such things as "no wanton violence, profanation of temples, looting, massacre, or conflagration" and excluded civilians as military targets. In modern times this qualification has produced such things as "the Geneva Convention," a somewhat futile attempt to delineate the rules to be followed in the conduct of some aspects of modern warfare.[8]

6) Augustine limited participation in warfare to professional soldiers, or those fighting in behalf of the government. And this was further limited to participation on the part of laypeople. No priests or monks, for instance, were to be allowed to fight. Theirs was a higher calling which separated them from the affairs of the world. Although the Protestant church claims to have broken down this distinction between clergy and laity, this same type of thinking is found in modern-day clergy exemptions from the draft.

7) Finally Augustine noted that the just war is one which is to be fought in a "mournful mood." The waging of war must be seen as a necessary, yet painful, duty which engages the Christian in a task

which is contrary to his peaceful nature. Thus, all feelings of hatred or revenge must somehow be purged from the participant.

This, then, in encapsulated form, is Augustine's position on the just war, a formulation which provided the framework, with few alterations, for later theorizing on this subject. It has come to us via the Reformation, where it was adopted by all the branches of the Protestant church with the major exception of the Anabaptists.

The Holy War

While this was the basic ethic followed during the Reformation, the crusading spirit of militant Calvinism also brought about a revival of the concept of the holy war. Bainton notes that this was partly due to circumstances, as the Calvinists in France, the Netherlands, Scotland, and England found themselves in the position of a minority faith fighting for survival; but it was also due to the ideal of the "holy commonwealth" which was represented in Calvin's attempt to "Christianize" Geneva.[9]

In the Netherlands this spirit was manifested in the revolt against Spanish rule which began in the 1560s and didn't officially end until independence was granted in 1648.[10] It was the Calvinists who provided the fighting fervor which William of Orange needed to realize the goal of independence from Spain, as was evidenced by his conversion to Calvinism in 1573.[11] This militancy was nurtured by the Protestant identification of Spanish misrule with Catholic religious tyranny, a viewpoint which was justified in light of Philip's introduction of the horrors of the inquisition into Dutch society.[12] What is important to recognize here is the not so subtle shift from just war principles to crusading principles which elevated the rebellion to the level of a war fought in behalf of the faith. The revolt against Philip II was fought by Dutch Calvinist forefathers in God's name. Bainton, in evaluating the Puritan revolution, which exhibited the same characteristic, lays down the following marks of a holy war:

> The crusading idea requires that the cause shall be holy (and no cause is more holy than religion), that the war shall be fought under God and with His help, that the crusaders shall be godly and their enemies ungodly, and that the war shall be prosecuted unsparingly.[13]

Unfortunately, the last requirement made itself felt in numerous brutalities which occurred on both sides during these religious wars. It is clear that in terms of Christian ethics, the crusading mentality operative during the rebellion in the Netherlands represented a regression from the just war position of Augustine.

These two approaches to war perhaps provide us with some insight into the minds of the first Dutch immigrants to America. Let us now examine how such principles worked themselves out in action by focusing on General Synod positions on this theme.

The Reformed Church in America and War

The American Revolution

In 1772 a document known as the "Articles of Union" was drawn up to put an end to a schism which had divided the Dutch Reformed congregations in the American colonies since 1755. Although they were still officially under the supervision of the Classis of Amsterdam in the Netherlands, this document allowed for the establishment of a General Body as the semi-autonomous authority for the colonial churches. Controversies over doctrine still had to be referred to the Netherlands, but this body was given the power to make decisions on local issues and to ordain clergy.

It was this rather young organization which found themselves meeting in 1775 only two days after the first blood of the Revolutionary War. Conflict had been anticipated for a long time before this, so when news of the fighting reached the members of the "Reverend Body" they were well aware of its implications. It reflected the seriousness of the upcoming conflict. Although no comments as to the justness of the revolt were made, the theme which would be consistent to this body's statements throughout the course of the revolution was clearly sounded, namely, that the bloodshed was the judgment of God upon the colonies for their "multiplied, aggravated, long continued, and unlamentable sins... called to repentance and conversion" (1755:57). This reflected the Reformed emphasis on the providential ordering of life. One can also pick up a strong covenant theme here in the sense that God's dealings with Israel in the Old Testament were seen to form the basis for his current relationship with the "New Israel" in the colonies.[14]

God's hand of judgment fell heavily upon the Reformed Church in the next three years, for the disruptions caused by the war made it impossible for them to meet. The extent of the damage done is sorrowfully recounted in 1778 when they were finally able to meet again. As in 1775, a strident plea for the confession and repentance of sins is sounded. This time, however, the "Reverend Body" has clearly taken sides. The statement of 1778 speaks of the disruptions caused by "the enemy," and God's blessing is invoked for "all classes in our land, both civil and military" (1778:65, 69). In fact, except for a staunch body of Dutch Tories in the lower counties of New York, the Reformed Church placed their loyalties firmly on the side of the rebels. As Luidens points out:

> the clergy of the Dutch Reformed Church were almost solidly in support of the patriotic cause, many contributing to the outcome, not only through patriotic sermons, but also through recruitment and by personal acts of bravery. Despite wide division in the areas adjacent to New York City, a very large majority of the Church members supported in various ways the cause of political independence.[15]

This loyalty was clearly expressed in 1780 when the General Synod Body drafted a "memorial" to be sent to George Clinton, then governor of New York, concerning "the Sins of the Land" (1780: 83ff.). In this statement the war is labeled "just and necessary," a war in which God has, "at diverse times and occasions, given the most indubitable proofs of his Divine and benevolent interposition for the soul of these United States." However, a favorable outcome of the contest depended upon God's favor which was directly linked to the state of morality in the colonies. Unless such sins as the profanation of the Lord's Day, swearing and "gaming" were dealt with in a more effective manner by the state, God's righteous judgment could change the "wished-for blessing into a curse." Thus, in the eyes of these pious Dutchmen, the balance of the war ultimately rested on the question of morality.

In summary it can be said that the "Reverend Body's" attitude toward the Revolutionary War was strongly influenced by Old Testament covenant parallels. God's righteous judgment was being exercised against his people (the elect in the colonies) by means of the British army. Thus, the sufferings and disruptions caused by the war were to be seen as deserved punishments for sin.

However, God would intervene in the colonialist's behalf if they would repent of their sins because their causes were just. In short, the "Reverend Body" gave justification to a war which, if not holy, at least involved the holy God in an active sense.

The Civil War

The General Synod's response to the Civil War presents us with an interesting blend of just war and holy war concepts. Already in 1861, just a few months after the surrender of Fort Sumter which signaled the call to arms, General Synod produced a statement which showed no reluctance to support a war which was being fought to buttress "the foundations of law and order, social, civil and religious" threatened by the Confederate rebellion (1861:10). It is important to note that the one issue which should have provoked the righteous indignation of the church, namely, slavery, is not mentioned. In fact, no mention is made of the slavery question until 1864, a full year and a half after Lincoln had issued his Emancipation Proclamation. It was the South's revolt against duly constituted authority which necessitated war, not their insistence upon holding slaves. Yet this was reason enough to sanctify the Union cause as one which "Christianity no less than patriotism" (1861:101) could applaud as just and necessary.

The statement of 1861 lays the foundation for what was to come, and provides us with the basic synodical themes which appeared during the five years of bloody civil war. They are as follows:

1) The war is the judgment of God. This repeats the theme which we found in statements on the Revolutionary War. However, it plays a smaller role here, and is not as concerned with enumerating individual transgressions.

2) The war is defensive in nature. It was the South who had provoked hostilities by rebelling against the government's rightful authority. This provided the justification for war.

3) The justness of the war calls for the full and unequivocal support of the church. It is here that just war and holy war concepts merge. Just war stipulations gave justification for Christian participation in armed conflict, but once this step was taken it was an easy second step to say that this was a war being fought for a righteous or holy cause. This kind of thought is reflected in the favorable comparison made between the heroic struggle in the Netherlands (which, as we have seen, exhibited the characteristics of a holy war and the Civil War).

4) Despite such sanctification of the conflict, it was to be fought in the spirit of Christian charity. In a resolution which echoes Augustinian thought on just war, synod said, "we cherish no feelings of bitterness, wrath, or hatred towards those who are unhappily arrayed against us, and utterly repudiate the spirit of retaliation and revenge as entering into the elements of this deplorable contest" (1861:101).

5) Finally, the members of synod express a desire for the war to remove the problems which caused it to occur and thus restore the peace so that "our prosperity for the future (may) be fixed upon an immovable basis." This again reflects just war mentality by its emphasis on a peaceful and constructive end to the conflict

Thus it can be seen that just war principles predominate in this early statement, despite an apparent sanctification of the war effort. However, while all these themes remained constant throughout the war, as the fighting intensified so did the emphasis on the righteousness of the cause. Already by 1862 the wickedness of the Confederacy was being contrasted with the righteousness of the Union which was "the best (government) enjoyed by the sons of men." Loyalty to the Union now became equated with loyalty to Jesus Christ, whose "cause of truth and righteousness in the earth" demanded unqualified support of the government's position. In addition, God's aid was invoked to bring victory to the Union armies, even though the ultimate end of victory was still seen to be the restoration of peace and harmony (1862:210-11).

This intensification of the righteousness of the cause shows how difficult it was to maintain the ideals of the just war in the midst of battle. To the credit of the synod, the first post-war statements call for "philanthropic and Christian efforts" to restore the South and pray for "an outpouring of (God's) Spirit on our scouraged [sic] and guilty land as shall heal the divisions, console the griefs, and remove the sins of the nation" (1865:648). However, in the same statement is a grateful recognition of the providence of God "whose right hand and whose holy arm have gotten Him the victory" (i.e., provided the Union with the strength to crush the wicked South). The holy war theme, hinted at in 1861, has now emerged as a predominant interpretation of a war which could be called anything but holy.

The war was dirty, grim, and grinding. New machines, and new fighting techniques wreaked a physical devastation unseen before. Commanders relied on reducing civilians to despair and crippling every kind of production as well as crushing the enemy's military force. Pounding artillery rockets, torpedoes, siege and unrelenting assault were all aimed at one goal: destruction. More men died in the Civil War than the total of all of America's other wars. The human damage was irreparable; the human attitudes remained unchanged.

The Spanish-American War

In April of 1898 President McKinley sent a message to Congress asking members to approve a war of liberation against the Spanish in Cuba. By July of the same year, Spain was suing for peace. General Synod met in June of that year. Thus their resolutions were framed in the short period of time in which America was involved in what Secretary of State John Hay called "a splendid little war."

The response of synod to this war presents us with a curious blend of pacifistic, just war, and holy war argumentation. The statement begins by condemning war "with its awful train of unspeakable horrors" as "the last resort of a Christian nation, which the boasted civilization of this latter day ought imperatively to forbid." The brutalities of modern warfare as exhibited in the Civil War had clearly made an impression. However, in a classic just war statement the synod sadly acknowledged that war "may become not only a stern necessity, but even the bounden duty of a people." This was the case in the conflict under consideration, for the oppressive nature of Spanish rule had forced the United States to use its military power to liberate the suffering Cubans.

At this point the statement goes one step further and declares: "In the application of this higher law, war may be a righteous act, and those who wage it may be acting in the Spirit of the Redeemer of the world, when he gave himself for man" (1898:256ff.).

Here we see once again the blending of just war and holy war concepts. It is fitting, in this regard, that this statement also refers back to the heroic deeds of Dutch forefathers who resisted Spanish rule "with courage unequaled and heroism unexcelled by the achievements of subsequent years."

Despite the "unspeakable horrors" of modern warfare, the synod of 1898 showed an inability to move beyond their past. In justifying war against Spain on humanitarian grounds (to right an injustice) the synod felt the need to go one step further and sanctify it as a holy war with the blessing of their Dutch forefathers.

It is true that the general tone of the statement reflects just war principles (i.e., war is a last resort, it should be fought only for the purpose of righting an injustice, its end must be constructive peace, etc.), but by saying that war "may be a righteous act" this synod exhibited an inability to move beyond the holy war mentality of their predecessors.

The important thing to notice is the moral struggle which was beginning to take place within the Reformed Church in America. For the first time a General Synod statement notes the true nature of warfare as a menace which unleashes "unspeakable horrors" upon humankind. However, this seems to have had little effect on the general tenor of their thought, for contained in the same statement is justification for war as well as its identification with the redemptive work of Christ. Such glaring inconsistencies could not last long in the face of the increasing ethical dilemmas posed by modern warfare.

World War I

On June 28, 1914, the fuse which ignited "the war to end all wars" was lit by the assassination of the Austrian archduke. The Western world was about to experience "war with its awful train of unspeakable horrors" in a way it had never experienced it before.

The General Synod's first response to the outbreak of hostilities reflected the overall reluctance of the American people to get involved in the war. Synod's moral and spiritual support was offered through their solidarity with the aims of the newly formed World Alliance of the Churches for International Friendship, but this meant little more than communication to European Christians their sympathy and prayer support.

Also included in these early statements, however, was a move toward what Yoder calls "the pacifism of programmatic political alternatives."[16] This type of pacifism, which was to play a more important role in post-war statements, looks for means other than war by which to solve conflict. In particular it looks to political solutions, or, in the words of the 1916 synod statement, "the substitution of judicial processes for war in the settlement of International disputes and the embodiment of these principles in National policies and laws" (1916:796).

This type of thought was little more than a reflection of the prevalent mood of the nation in the early stages of the war. President Wilson especially was convinced that a diplomatic solution could be found to the conflict. Unfortunately neither side would settle for anything less than total victory. By April of 1917 the pressure of events forced Wilson (as well as the Reformed Church in America) to acquiesce to this type of thought, and America entered the war on the side of the Allies.

The synod responded in character to the American declaration of war by affirming its loyalty "to a patriotism which has become sacred in this world-testing time" (1917:261-62). It should be noted that this was not a universal response in the United States. Thousands of Americans could not accept the decision to enter the war. The government, in fact, found it necessary to repress dissent in order to carry out their war aims, a repression which included censorship and jail terms for those who opposed governmental policies. Despite such suppression of opinion, however, a signifcant core of dissent survived throughout the course of the war.

Whatever the exertions of the Wilson administration and its supporters to silence the war critics, they never succeeded in convincing a significant minority of Americans that the nation's involvement was wise or just.

It may be that this questioning mood in the country toned down the response of synod to the war. Whatever the case, unlike previous synods' war statements, very little was said about "the cause." We can assume from the statement of loyalty in 1917 and the support given to those Reformed Church sons "following the Flag in Army and Navy" (despite just war discouragement of clergy-bound students to enlist) that the war was considered to be just. However, gone is the theologizing of earlier years which sought to involve God in the struggle. In its place is what appears to be a reticent yet firm acceptance of the "inevitable."

This reluctant acceptance of the American call to arms raises an important issue. Was this justification of another war due to an honest theological appraisal of the situation, or to an unwillingness to oppose national policy? This, in fact, is a question which could be asked of all the General Synod statements on war up to this point. Were they framed in a sincere attempt to apply just war specifications to governmental actions, or were they justifications after the fact, formulated in loyalty to the country, making it impossible to declare any war fought by America to be unjust? The statements themselves do not give us a definite answer to this question, but the rapid justification of war (in this case only two months after war was declared) seems to imply the latter.

Between the Wars

The appalling destruction of World War I, which in the eyes of millions of Americans accomplished little or nothing, brought in its wake two apparently opposite reactions—isolationism, which declared that America must remain free from all foreign entanglements, and internationalism, which called for moral involvement in every international dispute. Synod statements on the issue of war and peace during this period of time reflect the second point of view.

We have already noted that previous to American involvement in World War I synod pronouncements could be understood in terms of "the pacifism of programmatic political alternatives." What was a tendency before the war now became official policy after the war. As early as 1922 the principles of this approach to international conflict were delineated in a series of resolutions calling for the "substituting of INTERNATIONAL CONFERENCE AND GOODWILL for the age-old WAR method of settling international disputes" (1922:839ff.). The second resolution called for a "Committee on International Justice and Goodwill" to be appointed to serve as a liaison between synod and a committee of the same name on the Federal Council of Churches of Christ in America (the predecessor to the National Council of Churches). This committee was to serve as the conscience of the denomination on the issue of war and peace, not only during these idealistic days of international conference between the wars, but also during World War II.

The important thing to notice in this first post-war statement on peace is the ten point "confession of faith" of the Federal Council of Churches which was heartily endorsed by the Committee of Resolutions (and subsequently by the synod as a whole). Here we see the general thrust of post-war pacifism in what appears now to be a rather naive belief in the efficacy of international moral persuasion to enforce the peace. Synod's endorsement of the Pact of Paris in 1929 is a further example of this type of thought.

What appears to be naive today must have been perceived at the time as the only sane course to follow in a world which was sick of war. After "the war to end all wars" it was logical to assume that nations would do anything to avoid further bloodshed and destruction. In addition, it must be said that in terms of the Reformed Church's position on war, this represented a much more positive approach than what had been conceived in the past. Despite definite weaknesses which are inherent to this kind of pacifism, it at least reveals a willingness on the part of synod to search for workable alternatives to violence as a means of solving international disputes. As Yoder says in defense of such a position:

> If the claims of this programmatic approach are to be given a fair hearing, then we must project applications which would draw on the same resources in money, planning, and potential sacrifice of life which war can claim. "Nonviolence has never worked" is not a logically honest conclusion when there has never been a serious mobilization for it, with planning, strategy, thinking, and education like that the military does. . . When measured by such a fair test, in proportion to the cost of military methods in preparation and in lives if there were such a thing as a calculus of units-of-justice-per-cost-in-persons, it could certainly be argued that history's few hastily projected and poorly supported specimens of the nonviolent defense of justice have been no worse failures than the comparable violent alternatives.[17]

Unfortunately, the Western powers were not ready or able to resolve their differences in this manner. Only twenty short years after the signing of the armistice to end World War I international butchery began once again.

World War II

When General Synod met in June of 1939 the unthinkable prospect of another major war was becoming a reality. Hitler's war machine had rolled over Czechoslovakia in April, thus making a mockery of Chamberlain's ill-fated attempt to prevent war by appeasement and thereby discrediting in the eyes of many Americans the treaty approach to solving international disputes which had been adopted by synod between the wars. Despite this, however, the Committee on International Justice and Goodwill (hereafter referred to as the C.I.J. & G.) clung firmly to its conviction that war provided no answers to world problems. Thus, they continued their search for nonviolent alternatives.

The 1939 report of the C.I.J. & G. (which synod adopted) shows a depth of reflection on the issue of war which had not been present in previous synods. For instance, rather than the emphasis being placed on war as punishment for sin (although this was present as well) the report speaks of the waging of war itself as sin. This was an important new emphasis which could allow for a serious reappraisal of past positions on Christian participation in war. In addition, there is less readiness to put the church's seal of approval on anything the government deemed necessary. Reformed Church members were urged to beware of "false beliefs that lead to war," and to affirm that "No nation is all good or bad; so to believe is to foster injustice and hate" (1939:182ff.). This again shows a depth of reflection which exposes one of the serious shortcomings of a Christian ethic which justifies war. In order for war to be called just in the Augustinian sense of the word, one side must be in the right and the other in the wrong. By recognizing the complex web of guilt which is present in every conflict (but especially in international war), the committee helped lay the groundwork for later critiques of the validity of the just war theory for Christian ethics.

Also in this report is the first mention of an ideal which would be a pet theme of the C.I.J. & G. during the war—that in order to deal with conflict more constructively, a world government was needed (1940:543ff.). Narrow nationalism was viewed as one of the major causes of war. Therefore the time had come for one political system to rule the world. Only then could disputes be dealt with effectively.

Another major theme which appeared in 1939, and which came in the form of a recommendation from the C.I.J. & G., was a call for the Reformed Church to recognize the right of conscientious objection to war. The idea of conscientious objection was not new to synod, for clergy had always been seen to be exempt from participation in war (1940:545ff.). What was new was that it was now being extended to include laymen as well. The moral dilemmas posed by modern warfare had forced a significant minority within the Reformed Church in America to realize that participation in war could be in conflict with loyalty to Jesus Christ. Synod apparently agreed that such individual protest was valid, for they adopted this recommendation.

It is to the credit of the C.I.J. & G. that even at the height of wartime fervor they continued to support those Reformed Church in America members who took this unpopular stance. It also should be noted, however, that the acknowledgment of conscientious objector status did not represent a break from just war principles. On the contrary, it reaffirmed them. As Ernest Ruede says in discussing this aspect of the just war theory:

the ordinary citizen must obey his country's summons to participate in actual combat, unless he is convinced of the injustice of the war, and then he must refuse to participate in actual combat, even though he be sentenced to death for his refusal.[18]

By the time synod met in June of 1940 it was becoming apparent that America would have trouble staying out of the war. In the past year Hitler's armies had invaded Denmark, Norway, Holland, and Belgium, and were on the verge of taking control of France. The tension which this threat produced in synod is apparent in a resolution which was made at the close of its session. This resolution expressed deep sorrow and consternation over the tragedies the war was bringing to Europe. The "madness of this hour of destruction" clearly had had an impact on their deliberations. Despite the C.I.J. & G.'s clear call to stay out of the war, a pledge of loyalty to the government indicated that when the call to arms came, the Reformed Church was ready to justify yet another war (1940:681).

The war drums were beating even louder in June of the next year, yet the C.I.J. & G. continued to show a clarity of vision which allowed for no easy answers to the ethical dilemmas of Christian participation in war.

The teachings of Jesus have had no uniform interpretation on the subject of war; some have found justification for war in them, others have found utter denial of it. Whatever is the correct interpretation, history reveals that war is evil, that war violates human personality, and demoralizes social and political order. Hysteria is a regular accompaniment of war. Indeed, it is fostered and cultivated as a part of the method of leadership in wartime. Whatever a Christian's judgement as to participation in war, he must not link these facts. (1941:168)

This is a powerful statement, coming as it did on the eve of American entry into the war, and the fact that this report was adopted as a whole (even though the chairman had to point out that their committee was not properly labeled "pacifist"), shows that the committee echoed the sentiments of a majority of those present. If war was to be fought, and it appeared that it was, it was going to be fought by Reformed Church in America members in a "mournful mood."

The 1941 synod also reaffirmed its loyalty to the government "in this time of unlimited national emergency" (1941:325). Thus, although deeply concerned with moral implications of modern warfare, they were ready to support any course their country deemed necessary to restore the peace.

By June of 1942 the United States was fully committed to war. While synod produced no statement which justified the recourse to arms, it is clear that Christian participation in this war was seen as justified by all but a handful of Reformed Church in America members. There were only twelve conscientious objectors from the denomination during the war. The C.I.J. & G., therefore, changed tactics and focused on encouraging a positive end to the conflict.

> Our country is now involved in what has officially been designated The War of Survival. It is the high duty of this committee to remind the Christian Church that the survival of the national state is not the only end worthy of these times. Indeed, if some thing be sacrificed for the survival of National states alone, we shall most surely enter a new dark age of tribalisms and suicidal destruction. (1942:538)

This emphasis on a positive end to the cruelty of "necessary" methods, continuing support for conscientious objectors, and a stress on the need to "resist patent un-Christian attitudes" during the hostilities, became the predominant themes of this committee during the remainder of the war. All of these show that synod, with few if any exceptions, adopted these statements as its own, and was operating within the boundaries of the just war theory. In fact, it might be said that this was the first time in the Reformed Church in America's history that just war considerations were dealt with seriously. Yet at the same time this war also raised serious questions about the adequacy of the just war theory to deal with the nearly overwhelming moral dilemmas posed by modern warfare. How, for instance, could a war which "necessitated" massive slaughter of non-combatants as took place in the ceaseless bombings of European cities be called "just"? In their 1942 report the C.I.J. & G. declared that "War presents nations with terrible necessities" (1942:537ff.). Considering the brutal and dehumanizing nature of such "terrible necessities" during a war such as this, could the church in good conscience give its blessing to participation in it? These were some of the issues which synod wrestled with during the course of World War II. Their response made it clear that the days of easy justification of war were over. But it also showed that a reappraisal of traditional Christian responses to war was seriously needed.

The Vietnam War

The Vietnam War thrust the issue of Christian participation in war to the forefront of Christian reflections on morality. Like never before, this jungle conflict forced the Reformed Church (as well as every other denomination in America) to question long-held convictions about the place of warfare in the Christian ethic. Yet, interestingly enough, the debates which occurred within General Synod took place largely within the context of traditional just war thought. The war in Vietnam prompted deep soul-searching and brought some Reformed Church in America members to reject war in general as being antithetical to Christian practice. But the real issue at the time was whether or not this particular war was just.

In 1963 President Kennedy committed 16,000 American troops to South Vietnam in an "advisory capacity" to bolster an increasingly unstable regime. This began a series of commitments which intensified to the point where, by 1965, American troops were directly involved in the fighting. Once this step was taken the escalation of American involvement increased at a rapid pace.

Synod's first response to this new crisis in 1965 was totally in keeping with earlier positions taken on war. The increasing hostilities were viewed with consternation, but the responsibility of the United States to protect "the freedom and independence of all peoples," which of course included the South Vietnamese, was also affirmed. The main concern of synod at this point was that the negotiating table rather than bloodshed be used as a means to bring about a settlement of the conflict. The commitment to the goal of "the independence, freedom and self-determination of the people of South Vietnam" (the official rationale for military involvement), plus the addition of an amendment to the Christian Action Commission's report (the successor to the C.I.J. & G. or the social "conscience" of the Reformed Church in America) which commended President Kennedy for his "realistic approach to the practical issues in the problem of Vietnam," shows that at this early stage of the war synod felt the American presence in Vietnam to be justified (1965:221).

In 1966 a debate within the Reformed Church in America over the justness of this conflict was beginning to make itself felt.

Instead of seriously debating the issues, however, the Christian Action Commission chose to merely note that differences did exist. In keeping with the previous year's statement on Vietnam, their "suggestions" to the U.S. government reveal that they were unwilling to question seriously American involvement. Instead they continued to call for political solutions to the issues involved while at the same time attempting to apply just war conditions to the fighting, as is indicated by their request that the military avoid bombing population centers and attempt to keep civilians out of the picture (an impossible task given the nature of the conflict). In addition, the Committee on Overtures' addition to a separate recommendation requesting prayer for peace ("We would not favor peace at the price of tyranny. Peace without freedom is a contradiction.") (1967:126) shows a continuing commitment to official national policy.

By 1968 the ethical dilemmas posed by further involvement in Vietnam had become acute. During this year the bomb tonnage used against North Vietnam exceeded that used in both Europe and the Pacific during World War II. In addition, there were now over 200,000 American soldiers committed to the fighting and every day the horror of their participation was being brought home in technicolor to the American public via television news broadcasts. In light of this it is not surprising that the Christian Action Commission's statement declared the war to be unjust. This was done in a well-reasoned argument which showed the impossibility of achieving the declared purpose for the war. The main elements of this argument were then summed up in a recommendation which called the American government to disassociate itself from the fighting:

> Because there are firm grounds for doubt that continuation of the war in Vietnam will reach professed goals, and because of the terrible cost in human life and human suffering with its consequent brutal effect on our society, the General Synod adds its voice to those voices throughout the world calling for the United States to find at once a non-military solution in Vietnam. (1968:204)

The important thing to notice here is that this statement was framed strictly within the bounds of just war considerations. The Christian Action Commission had determined, based on the destructive evidence of human suffering and death in Vietnam, that the conflict did not meet the qualifications needed for it to be labeled "just." Their argument was not that all war is wrong, merely that this particular war was unjustified.

The die was now cast. For the first time in Reformed Church in America history an honest application of just war principles had given grounds for serious doubts about Christian participation in a war being waged by the United States government. It is probably true that those who opposed this point of view (of whom there were apparently a goodly number among the members of synod) also felt that there was justification for continuing the conflict. But it is more probable that the inherent conservatism of a deliberating body that stood in a tradition which had for the past 200 years justified every war that the United States fought made it difficult for some members of synod to break with this past. Whatever the case, from this point on the burden of proof lay squarely on the shoulders of the opposition.

The tension which this point of view engendered within synod is most clearly seen in the debate over the position of conscientious objectors within the fellowship of the church. In part two of the same report (1968:202ff.) a recommendation concerned with the right of the Christian to express "dissent from public policy" when he feels it to be in conflict with his loyalty to Jesus Christ was surprisingly defeated. It is surprising in light of the fact that during World War II, when there was little if any debate about its justness, this was an accepted position. One senses that the widespread dissent against public policy, which was being exhibited in the burning of draft cards and flights to Canada, posed a threat to a firmly held conviction which had been present in varying degrees of intensity in all previous synod pronouncements on war, namely, that loyalty to government was a duty incumbent upon all Christians, especially when that government is normally perceived to be "Christian" in its basic commitments.

The Vietnam War era witnessed widespread rebellion against such notions, and civil disobedience in the form of refusal to participate in an immoral war became "alarmingly" common. Thus it is not surprising that there was opposition to the Christian Action Commission's recommendations on conscientious objection as well as to their condemnation of American participation in the Vietnam War.

Without going into details, it can be said that this debate over the justness of the war in the face of reluctance to oppose national policy formed the backdrop for all synod pronouncements on

Vietnam from 1968 on. With hindsight we can say that events proved the Christian Action Commission to be essentially correct in their condemnation of the war. However, what is more important is to recognize that a precedent had been set. For the first time in American history General Synod, notwithstanding strong dissent, had used just war qualifications to stand up against government policy. Ten years later this kind of thinking was being disparagingly referred to as "the Vietnam Syndrome." Yet from the standpoint of Christian attitudes toward war it represents a positive first step toward a revival of the prophetic role of the church in a world which too easily justifies violent solutions to complex problems.

Conclusion: The Reformed Church in America and Peace

It is fitting that we conclude our study on the Reformed Church in America and war by taking a brief look at a document which helped inaugurate a new emphasis on nonviolence within our denomination (1974:222ff.).

In June of 1974, less than one year after the last American bomb had been dropped on Cambodia, the Christian Action Commission presented a report to synod entitled "The Church and a Witness for Peace." In essence this document confronts us with a critique of the type of mentality which had allowed synod to give their blessing to Christian participation in war for the first 170 years of American history. For example, while admitting that the just war theory offers "The best and most acceptable rationale for Christian participation in war," it also notes the danger that this could be taken as a license to support any war which our government may deem necessary. In this regard the report approvingly quotes Alfred Hassler as saying:

> There has never been an unjust war. Not for the people who fight on one side or the other, for those who support them. Men always justify their wars; otherwise they could not endure the suffering they inflict. In the name of progress. In the name of justice. In the name of the sacred nation. (1974:223)

With regard to what we have seen of previous synods' justification of war, such a critique is well taken. However, the call in this report for a basic reevaluation of the Reformed position on war in many ways merely echoes sentiments which had arisen periodically in synod pronouncements throughout the twentieth century. The difference is that we are now being asked to consider them from within the context of a position which is usually referred to as "pacifism." The writer of this report realized that such a radical break with Reformed tradition would not gain everyone's approval, for:

> To call upon the church to reject war as categorically as it rejects slavery may well upset those whose roots of faith are in nation and culture rather than in Christ, and it will disturb those whose main concern is to preserve something known as the "institution." (1974:224-25)

However, in light of what we know of modern warfare (or any kind of warfare, for that matter), in light of the destructive capabilities of the major world powers, but especially in light of the gospel by which we profess to live, it is difficult to see what other options we have.

IV
A History of Synodical Opposition to the Heresy of Apartheid: 1952-1982

Jack D. Klunder

There is an interesting scene that occurs in an obscure movie entitled *The Return to Oz* in which Dorothy meets and befriends a mechanical soldier who serves in the army of Oz. The mechanical man can do almost anything except, as the instructions point out, live. Now this mechanical man has three winding keys on its body: one for speech, one for thinking, and one for action. As these keys wear down Dorothy periodically has to rewind them. Suddenly, this mechanical soldier, "TicTok," has a bit of a problem: his thinking key has run down faster than his speech and action keys and Dorothy finds him making strange gestures and muttering strange utterances, all of which sound like much babbling.

Pumpkin Head (another friend) first analyzes the problem and shouts, "His thinking has run down but his talking is continuing!" to which Dorothy replies quickly, "Oh, it happens to people all the time."

Perhaps this scene adequately expresses what one feels living outside of South Africa and looking at the turmoil and unrest in that country. The tendency is to believe that the people's thinking keys have wound down while their talking continues. One has difficulty comprehending how a nation, founded upon Christian principles and dedicated to the purposes of the kingdom of God, could condone the evil and anti-Christian policies of the apartheid system of "separate and distinct." Is this different from the metal soldier in Oz whose thinking has run down but his talking continues? It is precisely here that the confusion multiplies. For it is evident upon deeper investigation that the thinking processes have *not* run down. As is the case in all instances of theological heresy, the thinking processes have been working overtime in an attempt to prooftext the heretical system and thus justify it theologically and exegetically.

What has been witnessed during the last decade is a country in the process of disintegration; a country which is not at peace with itself due to a severe and ingrained internal threat. Fear has embraced South Africa. Now, in the clutches of a civil unrest and with growing international censure, South Africa is experiencing the breakdown of its political system, a system that has not kept pace with the call for civil rights legislation. Though the American experience has been different in many ways, the lessons Americans are learning as they cope with their own racism may help them empathize somewhat with the situation in South Africa. The recovery of meaning cannot take place as long as the search rests on the morally corrupt and unjust system of apartheid. John Beardslee, in his first published article in *Neglected Arabia*, generalized on this problem with which the nations of the world cannot come to grips:

> [I would like to point out] that the history of our own country should show people that no amount of external civilization will bring a nation peace with itself—that "science" and "modern culture" without the deeper values of the Spirit are empty and unsatisfying, although they do not in themselves point out why they are so.[1]

Dr. Beardslee's observation coincidentally applies to the South African situation as well, and serves as a fitting introduction to the discussion offered here on recent relations with the South African churches.

This essay is concerned primarily with two matters. First, a historical survey is provided summarizing church statements and relations between the Nederduitse Gereformeerde Kerk and the Reformed Church in America. Secondly, the question of biblical and theological divergence is addressed in the context of the statements from the Nederduitse Gereformeerde Kerk in South Africa. Concluding the study is an excursus examining the propriety of the 1982 decision to suspend dialogue.

Beth Spring, in an editorial in *Christianity Today*, commented on the extremely close association between the church and the government in South Africa. She wrote:

> apartheid remains unique in today's world. It is officially sanctioned by the government and upheld by specific laws designed to keep the races separate. And it arises out of a world view shaped most explicitly by South Africa's Dutch Reformed Church. Through the church, apartheid was brought into being as a national policy in 1948. Many close observers of South Africa believe it is the church alone that holds the key to lasting change.[2]

Alan Paton, writing as a social historian, states that in spite of post-war reconciliation in the early 1900s,

> the Afrikaner still feared that he and his world would be swallowed up and lost in the great British culture. He also saw a danger that the traditional English policy of laissez-faire toward the black people might lead to his engulfment. So he again set about to re-establish his separateness and distinctness. He established cultural societies for the protection of his customs, history and language. And he succeeded magnificently, largely because of his fiery independent spirit, and also because the ballot box had been put into his hands by his British enemy. Thus emerged what is known as Afrikaner nationalism, the persistent and implacable urge that eventually, in 1948, defeated General Smuts, to the astonishment of every part of the civilized world.[3]

The church establishment, as part of the greater society of a nation, tends to lose its sense of purpose when it only is a reflection of the deep fears a people feel. The church can only be a causative institution as it points men and women to something greater than what society can offer. And this is only done through its prophetic voice in which it critiques the society on the basis of the Word of God. When the government and the church are so indebted to one another and so totally committed to the same cause, then God save the people!

For background purposes it will be helpful to set forth the Reformed Church scene in South Africa and provide dates for the establishment of the various branches of the church. It does get a bit involved and complicated and in the past has led to some confusion.

The Dutch Reformed Church was established in 1652 by settlers from Holland. Not until 1824 was a mission committee appointed to consider the needs of indigenous black people. In 1836 the first missionaries were commissioned. No less than five schisms occurred within the Nederduitse Gereformeerde Kerk between 1836 and 1866, mostly over the issues of native missions and political association with the British. The most significant schism led to the establishment of the Nederduits Hervormde Kerk (NHK). In 1859 the Gereformeerde Kerk (GK) was founded, separating mostly over doctrinal matters. Three other regional separations in the Orange Free State, the Transvaal, and Natal subsequently occurred but, in 1963, along with the Reformed body in South West Africa, these three churches reunited with the Nederduitse Gereformeerde Kerk (Mother Church) in what is known today as the General Synod NGK. The General Synod NGK along with the mission churches (separate churches serving black, colored, and Indian) are associated together in the Federal Council of Dutch Reformed Churches.[4]

A Brief History of Statements of the Reformed Church in America on Apartheid

There were five main statements issued during the thirty-two-year controversy (1950-82). The first of these, sent in 1950, contained an initial statement of regret over the church's stance on apartheid.[5] The second main statement was issued in 1967. Entitled, "Statement on South Africa," it appeared in the minutes of General Synod as part of the report of the Christian Action Commission (1967:211-12). It was this document that triggered the booklet, *A Plea for Understanding*, by W. A. Landman, a public relations spokesman for the NGK.[6] The third crucial statement came in 1976 when the Reformed Church in America entered into formal ties with other reformed bodies in South Africa (1976:228-29). The fourth important statement was written in 1980 by the Commission on Christian Unity (1980:147-51) in response to the booklet entitled *Human Relations and the South African Scene in the Light of Scripture* (hereafter referred to as *Human Relations*).[7] The last major statement was the 1982 synod resolution which suspended correspondence with the Nederduitse Gereformeerde Kerk (1982:136-39).

Prior to 1950: The Period of Cordiality

In 1950 the Reformed Church in America first made a formal statement to the Nederduitse Gereformeerde Kerk on the matter of apartheid. Prior to this initial correspondence the relations were cordial and fairly consistent. Edward T. Corwin states that the first reference to the Reformed Dutch Church in South Africa is in the minutes of General Synod of 1840.[8] Correspondence was thus opened with the South African Church and was mainly concerned with missionary efforts among the Dutch Boers (farmers). The Reverend David Lindley was sent as a missionary and subsequently joined the classis in South Africa in 1842. Further correspondence was exchanged regarding the intention to begin a theological seminary as well as an institute to train missionaries to work with the native Africans. Cordial greetings were exchanged throughout the middle of the nineteenth century and various committees were formed to offer help in some of these mission endeavors. *The Christian Intelligencer* (forerunner of *The Church Herald*) of May 24, 1859, described the opening of the seminary in Stellenbosch. The latter half of the century witnessed the continued cordial support of the sister churches. Resolutions in 1881 and 1897 can be read in Corwin's *Digest* in their entirety.[9]

Around the turn of the century the concerns from America centered in and around the Boer War (also called the South African War). The three-year conflict (1899-1902) between the Dutch Boers and Great Britain brought a wave of empathetic resolve from the Reformed Church in America. A resolution from General Synod in 1900 expressed "deep love and hearty sympathy to our sister churches of the Reformed faith in South Africa, which have suffered even to dismemberment" and called upon Great Britain "as the stronger power and as a Christian nation, (to) see her way (to) arbitrate the existing differences, and thus (bring) peace and prosperity to that desolate land."[10]

The war had long-lasting consequences as far as Afrikaner self-consciousness was concerned. And even though the end of the war issued forth a wave of goodwill in South Africa, as Alan Paton points out, "Reconciliation was not easily achieved."[11] Upwards of twenty thousand Afrikaner women and children had perished in the British camps, many of them of typhoid fever.

The Boer War was, indeed, a very important social component which helped shape the Afrikaner self-conscience not only affecting views on the various races but on society in general. The roots of apartheid had been laid early in the nineteenth century and the war fanned the flames of distrust and paved the way for a more thorough biblical and theological rationale for apartheid. Unfortunately, Reformed people in America were either unaware of the developing problem or unconcerned over it, for the record of General Synod shows no apparent opposition (and no knowledge of it) until it was firmly embedded in the political system. The extent of correspondence and exchange with the South Africans until 1950 is in the form of fraternal greetings (in 1926, 1934, 1936). A fraternal delegate was not sent until 1952, after the Reformed Church in America had become concerned over the policy of "separate and distinct."

Probably most striking to the first-time reader of the correspondence between the two sister churches is not the content of the message but rather the ignorance of both parties over the historical situations of the other. This ignorance led to a bland cordiality and then to confusion in more recent times. The overall lack of historical perspective from one body to the other is of crucial importance for understanding the church statements with respect to apartheid.

1950-1952: The Period of Education

The matter of the church's deliberate endorsement of apartheid was first called to the attention of General Synod in 1950 by the Classis of Ulster. Their words conveyed a spirit of love and concern for those oppressed by the apartheid system and called upon the Reformed Church in America to challenge the South African church to "give its witness and spiritual power to the solution of its aggravated problem upon the higher plane of Christian responsibility and Christian love for the least of these" (1950:117). The recommendation was considered by the Review Committee and it was suggested that the Committee on Resolutions write a "carefully worded communication to the Dutch Reformed Church of South Africa, expressing the deep regret of the General Synod at her endorsement of the program and requesting her to reconsider the action she has taken in this matter in the light of the Word of God" (1950:117). After review, the Committee on Resolutions presented the following communication which the stated clerk subsequently sent to South Africa.

MATTER CONCERNING
THE CHURCH IN SOUTH AFRICA

To the Reformed Churches of South Africa:

The one hundred and forty-fourth session of the General Synod of the Reformed Church in America, convened at Buck Falls, Pennsylvania, on this the 24th day of May, in the year of our Lord 1950, extends to you our most cordial greetings.

We have received with regret information of the segregation principle put into practice by your esteemed body in South Africa.

Feeling that we do not understand all the problems involved, nor the pressure of your practical situation, yet we are inclined through our deep love for you as a sister denomination of Dutch extraction to express our concern over the position you seem to hold toward members of the colored race.

We deplore the principle of segregation where ever it is practiced, especially in our own country.

Let us as disciples of Christ remind ourselves and you of the love of God that is shed upon the whole human family when He made us all of one blood in His own Image. Let us never forget that in Christ there is neither Jew or Gentile, bond or free.

We earnestly pray that the will of our Heavenly Father may become so clear and compelling that you may be led to the Christian solution of this great problem.

In the name of our Lord and Savior, we salute you and ask God by His Grace to make us all His humble and obedient servants. (1950:109)

Thus began the long series of formal complaints registered by the Reformed Church in America. The passage of time witnessed increasingly stronger language in the communication from America to Africa. But perhaps, most significantly for the Reformed Church in America, the South African crisis brought about the beginning of a process of racial introspection. Very early in their dealings with South Africa the Reformed Church in America began to realize that there was a log in its own eye that needed to be removed; and this log was nothing other than its own racist attitudes.

In 1952 the synod restated its opposition to the political system of apartheid, this time confessing before their brothers and sisters in South Africa that their complaints were issued "while humbly and penitently recognizing our own guilt in failing consistently to apply our Christian principles to race relations and problems in our own communities and nations" (1952:109). In response to the 1952 overture to General Synod by the Particular Synod of New York the Review Committee recommended the following resolution (which was subsequently adopted):

1. That Synod restate its conviction that racial oppression is basically unchristian in character and that the Church of Jesus Christ is duty-bound to speak the mind of its Lord on this issue;

2. That Synod express its profound regret that the situation in South Africa which, in the world press, has been closely associated with the Reformed Churches in South Africa, has placed the South African Reformed Churches and the great Afrikaans culture in a highly unfavorable light in world opinion;

3. That Synod express its conviction that racial oppression aids and abets Communism and does injury to the Church of Christ;

4. That Synod implore Almighty God to bless the Christian witness of our brethren in the Reformed Church in South Africa, to give them light, and to lead them out of their difficulty;

5. That Synod instruct its Stated Clerk to send a copy of this resolution to the Stated Clerks of our sister communions, the Reformed Churches, in South Africa. (1952:109)

1960-1961: The Period of Naivete

The Reformed Church in America was ready to take positive, supportive steps toward a just resolution of the segregation policy in South Africa and, rather naively, began the task assuming that it was only a blind spot in the vision of the South African church which needed to be enlightened. It would take a decade or more, however, before the Reformed Church in America finally realized that the basis of apartheid had been given theological foundations and that such biblical principles as reconciliation, church unity, and the oneness of the human race, commonly accepted (at least in theory in the Reformed Church in America) were not understood in the same light in apartheid theology. In this respect the discussion was naive because American theologians apparently did not recognize this disparity. On the one hand communications from America and Africa seemed to assume that both churches accepted without question a common understanding of the creation, differentiation of races, and church unity. On the other hand the continued defenses of apartheid coming from the Nederduitse Gereformeerde Kerk show in very clear terms that the South African theologians were acting in a manner consistent with their theological and biblical presuppositions. The discussion would only later turn to these presupposed underpinnings. In the decades of the fifties and sixties other approaches would be utilized.

There is a regrettable silence in the General Synod from 1952 to 1960, but in 1960 the whole matter comes to the fore again. The correspondence sent to the Nederduitse Gereformeerde Kerk in 1960 evidences the naivete spoken of above. The Reformed Church in America seemed to assume that the Nederduitse Gereformeerde Kerk had arrived at the doctrine of segregation uncritically. The letter says, "We have further stated our conviction that Christians who uncritically support these (segregationist) attitudes and practices do great dishonor to the Church of Jesus Christ and bring disgrace upon the integrity of the Gospel as it is proclaimed and lived." The Reformed Church in America was so certain of this that it went on in the letter to oppose those "who have clamored for your expulsion from the various councils of churches," a position which would be abandoned twenty-two years later (1960:291).

For the time being, however, the Reformed Church in America was content to work positively for reconciliation. This was evidenced in two ways: (1) through continued appeals for joint confession of sinful and racist attitudes, and (2) through prayer support.

As the church took these positive steps, ideas for a more aggressive policy of condemnation began to surface and, already in the decade of the sixties, divestiture in South Africa and the establishment of ecumenical ties with Christian fellowships other than the Nederduitse Gereformeerde Kerk were suggested. The naive phase of interaction came to an end somewhere between 1961 and 1967 (the Reformed Church in America's second period of prolonged silence on South African racism). When the issue was raised for the third time in 1967 the church would no longer be content to receive conciliatory correspondence from South Africa without a commitment to take a bold stance against apartheid.

1967-1982: *The Period of Action*

As was mentioned earlier, the Reformed Church in America used the occasion of racism in South Africa for some introspection. Those in the Reformed Church in America who made the effort to think through the problem realized that many of the same attitudes that were enshrined in the constitution of South Africa were just as prevalent in the United States and in their own church, albeit in more subtle ways. They further realized that it would be a terrible oversight to look aghast upon South African racism while ignoring racism in their own front yard. Hence a double-layered course of events began in 1967. At the deepest level was a renewed commitment to act in principle on its own racism in which prejudices, fueled by political power in the denomination, had subtly prevented minorities from entering the church or holding high positions; and, externally, the Reformed Church in America moved from the position of blissful ignorance of the South African scene and no longer would ride the fence. On the basis of Matthew 18:15-17, the Reformed Church in America had naively called attention to its fault. Now the witnesses would be called in and the wrong would be confirmed by the church universal.

In the history of relations between the two churches the report of the Christian Action Commission of 1967 is a key document in that it urged the Reformed Church in America to move from its position of relative passivity to one of action. It is quoted here at length because of its overall importance to the discussion.

Upon receipt of this document a letter was drafted by W. A. Landman of the Information Bureau of the Dutch Reformed Church in South Africa and sent to Marion de Velder, general secretary of the Reformed Church in America, and the General Synod, along with full documentation, and published as *A Plea for Understanding*.

STATEMENT ON SOUTH AFRICA

The Reformed Church in America has a special concern and responsibility toward South Africa. Our Church and the Dutch Reformed Church in South Africa are blood brothers, spawned by the same parents in the Netherlands. The continued endorsement by this South African Reformed body of the policies of the government toward eleven million black Africans is a cause of anguish, shame and embarrassment. Although no church or Christian, anywhere in the world, is guiltless in the matter of racism, the fact of failure cannot permit anyone who professes allegiance to Christ as Lord to remain silent. In any area of morality we must speak as penitent sinners, knowing that we fall below the mark of the high calling of Christ. But we see no expressions of guilt or penitence in the policies of the Republic of South Africa, nor do we see the Dutch Reformed Church assuming any leadership regarding the crimes against the non-white African. On the contrary, except for a few minority voices, the system of apartheid and oppression is condoned and justified.

Because of our concern for all people, we express our dismay over three policies of the Republic of South Africa—all of them interrelated.

1. The official policy of apartheid. Apartheid is nothing more nor less than legalized segregation, designed to keep the non-white African separate but unequal. There are many people who insist that America should clean up its own mess before it criticises anyone else. Segregation does exist in America in an alarming fashion. But there is a decisive and hopeful difference: the official policy in the United States is opposed to segregation and discrimination and the laws of the land are designed to crumble the barriers of prejudice. Not so in South Africa. In that land there is no hope for the future; racism is entrenched; the non-white African is doomed to an inferior status as second-class person. In the light of our faith as Christians there can be no justification for this. Trevor Huddleston in "Naught For Your Comfort" writes, "Any doctrine based on racial or color prejudice and enforced by the state is therefore an affront to human dignity and 'ipso facto' an insult to God himself. . . there is no room for compromise or fencesitting over a question such as racial ideology when it so dominates the thought of a whole country."

2. The policy of exploitation. Pharaoh's treatment of the Jews in Egypt was mild in comparison to the treatment of non-white Africans by the powerful white minority. No one

can deny that the white South African has been industrious, performed miracles in industrialization and achieved an unusually high standard of living. But the affluence of three million whites has been achieved at the expense of eleven million black people who fail to share the abundance or fruit of their labors. The Reverend Leonard Verduin, writing in *The Church Herald*, says "When we compare the standard of living among the whites (it is unbelievably high) with that of the non-whites (it is unbelievably low) the picture is not good. . . In one of the poorer 'localities' people are living on six cents a day for food! All skilled jobs are reserved for whites. Where whites and non-whites perform the same services, the former are paid up to four times as much. . . There is no limit to how little you can pay a black man for his services." An Amos would not last long in that land of exploitation if he dared cry, "Let justice roll down like waters and righteousness as a mighty stream!"

3. The policy of oppression. A system of legalized segregation and overt exploitation can exist only by the use of repressive measures. The government of South Africa has adopted the worst features of a police-state in order to maintain privileged status for the whites and to keep the non-white in subjection.

The non-white is refused his essential humanity and dignity as he endures the pass laws, the compounds, the denial of a voice in his own affairs, the right of speech, of assembly, of the right to petition, for redress of grievances. Arrest without charge and imprisonment without trial is common occurrence. Frederick Schwarz Jr. in "Christianity and Crisis," states that the totalitarian nature of the South African government "is the most flagrant example of an official policy of oppressing persons merely for the accident of birth." He cites the International Commission of Jurists as saying that the police-state legislation copies "the worst features of the Stalinist regime," in reducing the citizen's liberty to a degree not surpassed by the most extreme dictatorships of the left or right. Can Americans who talk so glowingly of freedom and liberty, who cry out against communist oppression, pass by on the other side as they witness the kind of oppression taking place in South Africa?

Mr. Schwarz, in the article quoted above, ends with this prophetic note: "Racism is too dangerous. A world divided into hostile camps could make the past conflicts over religion or ideology child's play. South Africa is a fuse that could set off racial conflict throughout the world. The United States must not sit by idly and let the fuse burn."

Trevor Huddleston makes this dire observation: "White South Africa will be fortunate if, fifty years from now, it is still a tolerated minority group allowed to remain where it has for centuries."

Because of its kinship with the Reformed Church in South Africa, because of its concern for all people, white and non-white, the Reformed Church in America must continue to appeal to the consciences of the Christians in South Africa calling upon them to reverse the patterns of racism and injustice. And because the time is short, we need to call upon the United Nations to take steps necessary to ensure justice for the oppressed and to aid victims of oppression. We need also to appeal to American businesses and industries to stop investing in South Africa. . . for business and profits, as usual, mean a subsidization of injustice. Those churches and organizations which have withdrawn funds from American banks involved in South African investment are to be applauded. The action may be little more than symbolic, but a faith which believes that "The foolishness of God is wiser than men, and the weakness of God is stronger than men" may find that the small moral gesture is the meaningful gesture. (1967:204-6)

Thus with this strong statement against the Nederduitse Gereformeerde Kerk the period of action had begun. The period of action lasted fifteen years and came to a conclusion in 1982 when the Reformed Church in America voted to sever ties with the Nederduitse Gereformeerde Kerk in order to stand more sympathetically with the oppressed in South Africa. During this period, however, significant things happened. One of the important events was the movement toward a policy of denominational divestiture in companies that carry on business in South Africa. Already in 1967 the Christian Action Commission recommended "That the Reformed Church in America support efforts being made to withdraw funds of church groups from those financial institutions which invest in South Africa" (1967:212). Although the synod voted to delete this item, the idea continued to surface and discussion of South Africa divestiture found its way into the synod record in 1978 (urged Reformed Church in America officers to study the question), 1979 (a brief description of Reformed Church in America holdings in thirteen companies that operate in South Africa), and 1980. In 1980, the General Synod voted for a total divestiture and communications were sent to all companies and banks with which the Reformed Church in America did business.

The second important action taken during this period was the establishment in 1976 of formal ties with other Reformed bodies in South Africa of black and colored background. By 1981 synod had taken the initial steps of engaging in direct ecumenical relations with the Dutch Reformed Church in Africa (black), the Dutch Reformed Mission Church (colored/mixed race), and the Reformed Church in Africa (Indian/Asian). Grants in aids, student exchanges and delegation exchanges were to be encouraged and carried out. A significant visit of Bishop Desmond Tutu was arranged through such efforts.

The third area of action concerns the correspondence with the governments of South Africa and the United States. The General Synod appealed to both governments in 1976 to work toward a just reconciliation and to restore peace in the riot-torn area of Soweto.

The fourth significant occurrence in the Reformed Church in America developed from the introspection that criticism of South Africa brought about. An ad-hoc committee on racism was formed by General Synod in 1964 but its responsibilities were assumed by other committees within a few years. At any rate, it is a good question what effect the dealings with apartheid theology had in the formation of the Black Council as well as the other minority councils in the Reformed Church in America.

The period of action came to a close in 1982, culminating with the suspension of ecumenical ties with the white church of South Africa. Thus began the fifth period, the period of alternate action, in which all attention was focused upon those who were waiting under the cross in South Africa. The final section of this study investigates some of the ramifications of that posture.

Biblical and Theological Considerations: A Look at the Correspondence from the Dutch Reformed Church in South Africa

The Basis of the Theological Divergence

As we study the responses of the Nederduitse Gereformeerde Kerk to the Reformed Church in America one thing is abundantly clear. The difference in racial orientation arises out of their respective points of view on God's will for his creation in respect to race differentiation. The question reduces down to this: Was it the will of God that races of people remain distinct and separated so as to pursue their own destinies before God, and, in that pursuit, to reflect his glory? To this question the Reformed Church in America was ready to enter an unqualified negative. But the Nederduitse Gereformeerde Kerk apparently was equally convinced that God had willed separate races, expected them to remain distinct, and had ordained the church in South Africa in the fulfillment of this mandate. Hence the accusations of exploitation, oppression, and racism were, in their opinion, the product of misinformation by subversive liberals who did not understand the scriptural mandate.

Source Materials

Two major pieces of literature have been made available to the Reformed Church in America which contain the biblical rationale for the church's support of apartheid. It is from these two sources in particular that this section has been prepared. These two publications must be considered as primary and foundational church statements of the Nederduitse Gereformeerde Kerk. *A Plea for Understanding* was prepared as a reply to the Reformed Church in America by Landman. It was prompted by the letter of disapproval from the General Synod of 1967 which also included the official "Statement on South Africa." *A Plea for Understanding* is an attempt to call upon the Reformed Church in America to be better informed on the situation of interracial relations in South Africa and includes numerous annexes which attempt statistically to justify apartheid.

The other publication, entitled *Human Relations and the South African Scene in the Light of Scripture*, was published in 1976 and serves as a biblical defense of the ecclesiastical-political relation. The book is a record of synodical legislation of 1974 and "represents the convictions existing in the Dutch Reformed Church with regard

to the problem of relationships in a multinational country, as seen
from the point of view of the eternal and immutable norms of the
Word of God."[12]

Together these two statements give the sociopolitical and the
biblical-theological rationale for the policies of apartheid.

Primary Passages of Scripture under Scrutiny

As was mentioned earlier, the question of singular importance
here is whether or not it was the will of God that races and peoples
(and their destinies) remain separate and distinct in order to pursue
God along national, individualistic pathways. For if it is accepted as
a normative principle of Scripture that God's will is for separate
development, then even such a passage as Ephesians 2:14, "For he
is our peace, who has made us both one, and has broken down the
dividing wall of hostility," is interpreted in a different light. Bishop
Desmond Tutu, in a powerful essay entitled "Apartheid and
Christianity," speaking to this very issue, wrote, "Apartheid
maintains that human beings, God's own creatures, are
fundamentally irreconcilable, flatly contradicting the clear
assertions of Scripture that God was in Christ reconciling the world
to Himself. Apartheid is, therefore, a heresy."[13]

The Ideal of Apartheid

Perhaps it will be helpful to have clearly in view the goal of
apartheid. For it is of utmost importance to acknowledge the fact
that the Nederduitse Gereformeerde Kerk is not indifferent to
problems of justice, self-determination, self-government, and
human rights. It has, however, concluded to its own satisfaction,
that racial integration and conjoint government in South Africa is
not in the best interest of the white minority nor in the best interest
of the various tribal-national groups in South Africa. While
Americans may debate the question of whether or not equality
under the law is best attained through integration of the races or
segregation into numerous groupings, at least we must be clear on
the ideal of apartheid: its purpose is to separate people into
nationalities, relocate them to the appointed reserve (called
Bantustans), and turn over to them the responsibility of self-rule.
These separate states may then pursue what the 1960 synod called a
"Policy of independent, autogenous development." The stipulation
was that the state must see to it that the policy is applied in a fair

and honorable way, without affecting or injuring the dignity of the person. Then, associated together in a purely economic way, these self-governing nations would assume a type of commonwealth relationship to one another. Then, as separate nations joined in a loose confederacy, the biblical principles of fairness, justice, and peace would come to bear upon each individual.

The Tower of Babel (Genesis 11:1-9)

It is the clear intention of *Human Relations* to prooftext the presupposed thesis that separate development of peoples is the will of God. Herein is a wonderful example of how not to interpret Scripture; that is, to begin with a premise or principle and then turn to the Scripture to prove it or discredit it. The Nederduitse Gereformeerde Kerk attempts to prove the principle of separate development, not by showing that it is assumed all through the Bible but rather by proving that the Bible does not disallow it.

The argument is set forth from Genesis 1:28 where Adam and Eve receive the divine mandate (which is also to all humankind) to "be fruitful and multiply, and fill the earth. . . and have dominion over [it]." The point here, rightly stated in the report, is apparent: it was the will of God that his whole earth be inhabited. However, the next thing that happens in the report is quite curious. An assumption apparently is made that the filling and inhabiting process was taking too long and God was displeased with the delays. In order to hasten the process the Lord confused the language at Babel, and the result was that meaningful communication became impossible. Apartheid theology asserts that these language groups, from then on, associated together and went their separate ways to fill the earth. Thus the divine act at Babel, which manifested itself in the diversification of the human race, is viewed not as a punitive measure by God, but rather as an act of mercy to assist the human race in fulfilling the creation mandate. This the report states very clearly:

> Ethnic diversity does not have a polyphylogenetic origin. Whether or not the differentiation process first started at Babel, or whether it was already implicit in the fact of Creation and the cultural injunction (Genesis 1:28), makes no essential difference to the conclusion that ethnic diversity is in its very origin in accordance with the will of God for this dispensation.[14]

Now the question occurs: Is this really the chief emphasis of the Babel story? That is, does this account of the confusion of tongues at Babel indicate that autogenous development was God's will? The response of the Commission on Christian Unity was that this account was clearly not recorded in Scripture to indicate autogenous development as God's will but rather to show God's disapproval of man's pride and arrogance which led to the building of the tower. Quoting S. R. Driver's commentary on Genesis, the report states that the Babel story is an account of "the penalty for misdirected ambition" (p. 148). This account was not an explanation of the divine origin of various races. Language was confounded and this had nothing to do with skin color or nationality. To assume that this event represented anything but a divine punishment was to totally disregard the intention of the text. Here is, in capsule form, a reiteration of a major biblical theme, "a bit of cultural history in which man's rebellion against God becomes evident and in which God's judgment takes place!" (G. von Rad, "Genesis," p. 147) (1980:149).

In the conclusion (section 9.3) of *Human Relations* another rather curious point of view comes to the fore. Apparently, in the Babel experience apartheid theology does not see a rebellion of man against God but rather a humanistic attempt at unity, of which God wishes to have no part. This then forms the basis for understanding the call of Abraham and the formation of the Israelite nation. This further places apartheid theology at odds with Reformed orthodoxy for it does not recognize the full religious significance for the calling forth of the Hebrew nation.

Acts 17:26

The report of the Commission on Christian Unity then goes on to further challenge the Nederduitse Gereformeerde Kerk's interpretation of Acts 17:26 and the account of Pentecost, both of which were employed by the Nederduitse Gereformeerde Kerk to give credence to the Babel account. While affirming that "the New Testament does not question or abrogate the equivalence and solidarity of peoples" and that texts such as Matthew 28:19, Acts 2:5, and Romans 1:16 simply presuppose the real fact that there is diversity in the human race, the report goes one step further (again, based upon its overall desire to prove a pre-concluded thesis) to assert that this diversity is God's will (1980:149).

Acts 17:26 is cited in favor of this unwarranted conclusion. Paul, preaching on Mars Hill in Athens, states that the sovereign God "who made the world and everything in it" (verse 24) also is sovereign over "every nation of men. . . having determined allotted periods and the boundaries of their habitation" (verse 26). The report then observes that the New Testament assumes the existence of various nations "but never characterized it as sinful; nor does it call upon Christians to renounce their nationality" (1980:149).[15] Evidently there has been a serious confusion of terms and an unwarranted identification has been drawn between races, language groups, and nations.

Implications of Apartheid Theology's Interpretation of the Creation Mandate

Although the implications of apartheid theology are many and varied, in the interest of space only three areas are identified where the disruption is especially glaring. These include the need for a prophetic voice in the area of social justice, the mission theology of the church, and marriage and family life.

Social Justice

It is the contention of *Human Relations* that social justice is a high priority on apartheid theology's agenda of issues; that autogenous development is an acceptable method of insuring social justice for all national-racial groups in South Africa. This emphasis appears to be in response to the continued challenge from the Reformed Church in America to defend itself biblically in the area of social justice. In South Africa the issue of social justice is especially relevant in the areas of fair employment for all people, the preservation of native culture and values, self-determination and representation in government, individual human rights, education, migrant labor, the intention to develop Bantu homelands, and the question of non-native, non-white groups such as Asians, Indians, and coloreds. *Human Relations* does not attempt to resolve these issues; it only raises the questions and gives information regarding the complexity of the situation. Indeed, the situation is complex especially when approached from the non-integration, separate development stance of apartheid theology.

Comparing *Human Relations* with *A Plea for Understanding* it is quite evident that the former document gives a more realistic

picture of the challenge facing the church. The latter attempts to
justify apartheid by showing that the non-white groups do not have it
all that bad; that justice is being done in and through the
resettlement option. But *Human Relations* readily admits problems
that will not vanish even if resettlement were to be successful. The
following quotations are from section 56 of the report.

The following problems deserve continued attention, study
and action on the part of state and church:
1. Uncertainty about the Coloureds' political and
economic future, which leads to indifference and
frustration, and militates against the cultivation of a will to
self-development.
2. The injudicious proclamation of some group areas
which cause inconvenience and even privation among the
Coloured people.
3. A serious situation has arisen in certain Coloured
residential areas as a result of an inevitable delay in the
provision of community and recreational facilities after
housing schemes have been completed.
4. Dissension in the Coloured community hinders and
prevents clearly formulated viewpoints.
5. The admixture of Bantu with Coloureds creates a very
serious problem in many instances.
6. The wage gap between Coloureds and Whites doing the
same work with the same degree of responsibility creates
bitterness and a sense of injustice among the former.
7. The problems caused by the abuse of liquor are among
the most serious social evils demanding the continuous
attention of the church.
8. Another problem demanding the serious attention of
the church is the need for family planning and the
combating of immorality and promiscuity which cause an
extremely high illegitimate birth rate.
9. The uncontrolled influx of large numbers of Coloured
to certain areas creates problems in both housing and labor
relations which render the overall problem more acute in
certain respects.
10. Finally, there is the uncertainty among Coloureds as
to where they belong as a group.[16]

Missions

The indoctrination of apartheid also evidences itself in the area of missions. The Nederduitse Gereformeerde Kerk is a mission-minded church and is, apparently, committed to the task of establishing indigenous congregations. However, the conviction of the necessity for strict separation of peoples overrides the biblical mandate for unity in the church. The result is a vision of diversity in which congregations remain unique in their racial-ethnic compositions. Thus within a given locale there will be any number of congregations, each with a singular purpose for separate existence, namely, the obligation to serve its own kind.

Here note must be taken as to the exegesis of certain key texts: Matthew 28:19, Acts 2:5, and Romans 1:16. Each of these texts makes passing reference to the real fact that various nations do, indeed, exist. However, without qualification the conclusion is drawn that it is God's will that the church be as diverse as the nations of the world. This is what is explained in section 60 of the report under the statement, "The Christian faith is universal: it is our duty to localise its universality." This is further spelled out in such statements as: "The natural diversity of man and people survives in the Church of Christ but is sanctified in him." Consideration is apparently not given to the possibility that the church, being "in" the world but not "of " the world, may mean that it is called to a higher plane of unity and trust than what is observable in the world. Perhaps the natural barriers of linguistics, culture, and race—those things that diversify the human race—are to be overcome through the dynamic intervention of the Holy Spirit, who makes all things new (Revelation 21:5), who, in peace, makes us all one and breaks down the dividing walls of hostility (Ephesians 2:13-16). And while it is true enough that Paul "came as a Jew among Jews to win them over" is it not of equal importance that he soon went to the Gentiles to win them over? Acts 11:12 describes a similar circumstance (Peter speaking): "And the Spirit told me to go with them [three Gentile converts] without hesitation." Later in that chapter a scattering of the faithful is described, which has nothing to do with the so-called natural diversifying factors, but rather occurred due to persecution (11:19ff.). The new name given to the band of believers in Antioch—Christian—is generic. It encompassed both Jews and Gentiles.

Marriage

The issue of marriage between persons of different ethnic and/or racial groups—miscegenation—evidences yet another area in which the "separate and distinct" philosophy of the apartheid system has overriden general biblical guidelines. For while admitting, on the one hand, that "Scripture neither directly prescribes nor prohibits racially mixed marriages," the Nederduitse Gereformeerde Kerk, on the other hand, believes that a normative point of view may still be found in the Bible. Here is where the "separate and distinct" philosophy overrides: for if it is a foregone conclusion that God's will is for the continuation of diversity of national, ethnic, and racial groups, then it only stands to reason that mixed marriages are not in accordance with his will. Apartheid theology thus holds the church has a "pastoral" responsibility to speak against miscegenation, and the state, in order to "jealously guard the spiritual and cultural treasurers" of the differing national groups in South Africa, has the right to "prohibit the contracting of such marriages. . . to preserve order in society. . . when it decides for certain reasons that in a multiracial and multinational society public order is best preserved by the separate existence of the various population groups, or when the government is convinced that public order is threatened by the contracting of mixed marriages."[17]

A Final Observation on the Decision of the Reformed Church in America to Suspend Dialogue with the Nederduitse Gereformeerde Kerk

The General Synod of 1982 resolved: "To inform the Nederduitse Gereformeerde Kerk in South Africa of the intention of the Reformed Church in America to pursue further dialogue only when the Nederduitse Gereformeerde Kerk renounces Apartheid and enters into conversations on an equal basis with other Reformed Churches in South Africa" (1982:139). The Advisory Committee adjusted the wording in an attempt to make the action more positive in its intention. The synod conveyed that it was committed to dialogue but only on the two conditions that apartheid be renounced and conversations be opened with other Reformed bodies in South Africa. Neither condition was met. The result in South Africa has been a steady increase in social unrest and political oppression. Now, in retrospect, the propriety of this decision to suspend ecumenical ties can be historically examined. It is a most serious matter; for with the eyes of the world upon us, the Reformed Church in America has dealt decisively with an erring member.

The Reformed Church in America recognized certain obvious factors that led to the breaking of ties. First, there was the fact that the vast majority of Christians in South Africa were non-white, and oppressed by the apartheid system. Secondly, justice and truth were clearly on the side of the non-white, half citizens who were waiting and hoping for liberation. Thirdly, the Reformed Church in America clearly had a moral duty to stand with these brothers and sisters in their struggle, to support them, encourage them, pray for them, and work with them to dismantle the unjust system that oppressed them. Lastly, the church had a further duty which was to pray for the oppressors, to continue to speak the truth in love, and to ceaselessly call upon them for a peaceful resolution and joint confession of racist attitudes. If there is an area where the Reformed Church in America can be faulted it is at the point of failure to "pray for those who persecute you" (Matthew 5:44).

The Reformed Church in America must be very clear on the deeper issues that have brought white South Africa to this point of blindness, namely, the psychological fear of engulfment and anxiety over its threatened survival. South African racism has grown up over centuries of time; and mere dialogue has proven ineffective at stemming the rising tide of racism. Racism thrives when fear and ignorance combine forces. South African racism is evidence of the tremendous and ingrained fear of social engulfment. Thus we come to see that the political oppressor of millions is itself oppressed psychologically by its own deep-seated fears and anxieties. Ideally, it would be nice to think that the Reformed Church in America could, on the one hand, work along with those who work to dismantle the apartheid system and, on the other hand, help the oppressor overcome its racist attitude. The problem is that dialogue with the oppressor is so readily misconstrued as acquiescence. The heresy of apartheid had created a chasm of suspicion which demanded a decision to stand on one side or the other. To straddle the chasm was to ignore the responsibility of solidarity with the suffering millions who could not afford the luxury of continued dialogue. Thus the breaking of ecumenical ties was the strongest statement the Reformed Church in America could make to the oppressor and the most beneficial action toward the oppressed.

Hopefully, the show of solidarity with other churches, the continuation of economic sanctions, and the voicing of displeasure to the governments will help bring about a satisfactory solution to this terrible evil of apartheid. We in America must remain as concerned about the ethics of means as we are about the desirability of ends. The means must conform to the standards of God's Word as strictly as do the ends; and the virtues of peace and justice must prevail in the means even as they do in the ends. The Reformed Church in America must continue to pray that God Almighty will open the eyes of those in South Africa who are blinded by their fear and pride. And we must have a message for the Nederduitse Gereformeerde Kerk: there is an identity beyond apartheid, and shared government and integration will not lead to social engulfment and cultural loss. The church is to be emphatically different from the nations of the world; there is to be peace and unity. In the church the discord and diversity of the world is not to be imitated but overcome. This is the glory of Christ.

V

The Origins of the Theological Library at New Brunswick

Russell L. Gasero

The Dutch Reformed Church was under the care of the Classis of Amsterdam from its establishment in 1628 to its initial independence in 1772. By the first third of the eighteenth century, it was recognized that the cost of educating and ordaining ministers in the Netherlands was too great, both in money and lives. The Dutch Reformed Church had always required an educated clergy, and the Classis of Amsterdam was concerned that this traditional requirement not change in the church in America.

By the mid-eighteenth century the American ministers had split into two bickering groups—the coetus and the conferentie. The coetus was a group of ministers who favored independence from the mother church in the Netherlands and sought to establish their own college and seminary in this country. Led by members of the Frelinghuysen family, they finally received permission to establish Queens College (now Rutgers University), securing its first charter in 1766. The conferentie opposed the idea of an independent classis in America and the severing of ties with the Classis of Amsterdam. Members of the conferentie had undertaken efforts to secure a chair of theology at the emerging Kings College (now Columbia University) in the 1750s. However, with the establishment of Queens it was clear that the Dutch Church would also be establishing its own chair of theology in this institution.

The Revolutionary War interrupted the plans of the coetus group (by this time merged again into a united church) for the formation of a theological institution, but ultimately they were successful. The church declared its independence from the Classis of Amsterdam prior to the Revolution and this was formally recognized by 1792. During this period the Reverend John Henry Livingston successfully brought the two opposing factions back together into one unified body and thus earned the title of "Father of the Reformed Church in America."

Efforts to establish a theological institution continued during the Revolution, and in 1784 the Reverend Livingston was appointed the first professor of theology by the General Synod and the Reverend Hermanus Meyer was professor of the sacred languages. While they each operated in their own parishes for a time, it was clear that synod, in light of their acceptance of the tradition of a well-educated ministry and the style of theological education in the Netherlands, did not intend to develop a system of internship under a practicing minister, but rather desired to establish an institution for theological education. The seminary had considerable financial difficulties in its earliest years when Livingston was located in New York and later in Flatbush, Brooklyn. It began to achieve solid footing after Livingston located in New Brunswick in 1810. It is at this point that the account of the development of a theological library starts.[1]

Establishing the Library

The history of the establishment of the theological library is a story of success and failure, and ultimately, success. Like many of the institutions started in the Reformed Church, there was a great deal of initial interest in the project, but when the time to contribute funds arrived, interest seemed to wane. The development of the library parallels the history of Queens College.[2] The early years were fraught with anxiety about the existence of the library and its adequacy for the support of an educated clergy.

After Livingston was appointed professor in 1784, it is probable that students used his own personal library and sought to borrow or purchase whatever additional volumes they needed. The General Synod in 1787 appropriated fifteen pounds for the purchase of books which would be used by the students studying with Livingston (1787:157).[3] The students were having difficulty obtaining the necessary textbooks and synod felt some obligation to offer a rudimentary library for their use.

There is no mention in the report of the professor of theology to the General Synod regarding the necessity of a library prior to his move to New Brunswick. Nor does there appear to be any concern on the part of synod to offer more than token assistance for obtaining hard-to-find textbooks. Of course, the church had only recently weathered the storm of the American Revolution and money was scarce for many of its programs.[4] The effort to sustain a new college and provide a firm foundation for theological education left little opportunity or resources for a library. Given the small size of the church and the small number of students studying for the ministry, it is obvious why the creation of a library did not seem to be a pressing need. However, General Synod did take notice of the need of a library in the context of the total institution, for while seeking to support a professor of theology on the faculty of Queens College, synod agreed "to provide money for its purchase of a theological library, and for the purpose of erecting a theological hall" (1807:366). Livingston reported in 1812 that neither the library nor the plans for one had yet been undertaken. In fact he noted that there were insufficient funds to support a professor, and no provision for obtaining a library. The students, on their part, deplored the lack of a theological library and were saddened by the deficiency of books available for their use (1812:416).

Livingston seemed to be aware of this need and kept in mind the building of such a library in the future, when financial conditions were better. He worked toward securing a collection of books which would serve the needs of theological students, for in 1794 he was instructed to take all the books he had procured and prepare a catalog. These volumes would then be available to the other two professors (Reverends Romeyn and Froeligh) upon their application to Livingston for the needed volumes (1794:258). His concern and the manner of his reports to synod resulted in some quick action, for some years later the committee on the professorate reports that "a responsible library has been collected in Queens College" (1813:37). The majority of these volumes which established the library came by donation while a few additional ones were purchased. That year the Board of Superintendents had appropriated $100 for the purchase of books (1814:19).

During this period a pattern was established which was to continue for the next decades. The concern of Livingston and the students' expression of need was strong enough to cause synod to authorize a collection to be made in all the churches, one-half of which would be used for the procuring of a library "among other things" (1812:429). A committee was appointed and consultations were begun with the Board of Trustees of the college to determine the library needs of the school.

Enquiries were made each year as to whether churches had contributed funds. Donations of both books and money were gradually received and the library slowly grew. General Synod continued to appropriate $100 for books. Perhaps these slow beginnings and limited finances were for the ultimate benefit of the library. In one sense it enabled General Synod to put before the whole church the need for a library and at the same time to explain why a respectable collection was important. Thus, the awareness of the congregations was increased toward scholarship and study centered in a denominational library. In 1815 the General Synod agreed to appoint "pious and active men within the bounds of each classis, or congregation, to solicit annual subscriptions, to the amount of 50 cents or more, from each subscriber" (1815:42). Forty-nine individuals were appointed and instructed to visit every family in their classis (they were paid a commission of seven percent for their efforts). Thus, the problems of the school and the library were brought home to nearly every member of the church.

It appears that this committee was successful, for the 1820s saw an increase of donations of both private libraries and funds. As a result General Synod, in 1818, sought "to appoint some person or persons to have charge of the Library, under such regulations as the Professors may make; and the same or some other person purchase books for the Library" (1818:52).

Awareness of the library's needs was increased, but synod was still reluctant to invest heavily in building up a large collection. During the period 1815 to 1825, synod had spent over $700 on volumes to establish the library and had received a number of donations of books as well. However, the financial stability of the schools was still uncertain and synod was not interested in appropriating significant funds for the purchase of a theological library. But when Colonel Rutgers placed Queens out of financial jeopardy in 1825 with his generous contribution, the attention of the General Synod was again turned to the development of a satisfactory library for both institutions. Once again they appointed agents to solicit funds for the increase of the library. A group of twenty-nine individuals was appointed (1825:29).

This time their work was far more successful, for the library began to increase at a steady rate in the following years. Initial subscriptions led to the purchase of bookcases and about 130 volumes which included a complete set of Calvin's *Works*, Hale's *Chronology*, and Quick's *Synodicon*. At that time the church began to think of the role and function of the library in the life of the college and the denomination. The library was seen as an essential part of both schools, indeed, it "has become an item of special importance and is deemed of great importance to the prosperity of the Literary and Theological Institution" (1828:68). This was reaffirmed once again in 1829, and the synod was now seeking $1,600 for the increase of the library (1829:197).

Awareness of this need led to some significant offers during the next two decades. Dr. Selah Woodhull's library was purchased by the school in 1826. Dr. Woodhull was professor of ecclesiastical history in the seminary and professor of metaphysics and philosophy of human mind in Rutgers during the period of 1825 to 1826.

In 1832, the school undertook to purchase the library of the recently deceased Dr. John De Witt. De Witt had been professor of ecclesiastical history from 1823 to 1831, as well as oriental literature from 1825 to 1831. In Rutgers, he was professor of belles-lettres, criticism, and logic from 1825 to 1831. His library was appraised at a value of $2,104.59, and this excluded a collection of 200 Dutch volumes. (But this library did include an edition of the Robert Stephens Greek Testament in folio of 1550.)

Unfortunately, General Synod had a narrow view of the needs of a theological library and the scholarly interests of the student body were none too lofty. Synod stated that, "with respect to the Dutch books included in the library, although your committee have no doubt but that many of them are intrinsically valuable, yet as very few of our students, for those whose benefit this library has been purchased, could make any use of such books, they are of opinion considering the state of the Synod's funds, that no allowance for such books should be made" (1832:102).

This was an interesting statement considering what the future course of the library's development was to be. Through no planned program of acquisition, the seminary library would become, in just a little more than fifty years, one of the finest repositories of Dutch books in the country, and this would be seen as one of its major strengths. Nevertheless, De Witt's library was acquired with Dutch volumes, and Mrs. De Witt was finally paid in full in 1835. This sizable acquisition necessitated the need for a catalog and the first printed one was published in 1832.

The next fifteen years saw a steady rate of growth through purchase and donations. In 1839 the library obtained Fox's *Book of Martyrs* in three volumes folio. In 1844 a number of volumes in Latin and 146 Dutch volumes were donated by Reverend Zachariah Kuypers. Thus, a strong collection in the classics and in Dutch theology and literature was developing. Most of the acquisitions were libraries of deceased ministers whose families had little or no ability to read either Dutch or Latin. Finding little use for these books they were quite content to donate them to the seminary, especially if a small sum could be paid to help alleviate the suffering of a poor widow. During this period, the manuscript collection of the library also began to develop. Livingston's lectures were gathered and bound for deposit in the library (1833:164).

The operations of the library were beginning to become formalized and the school began to think about proper care and custody of an increasingly valuable collection of books. In 1842, the president of the college reported:

> It is feared that books are lost and injured to an extent far greater than is imagined by those who have not closely examined the matter. The frequent changes rendered necessary by the appointment as librarian of a member of the seminary, will always lead to loss and confusion. I would respectfully recommend the appointment of a permanent officer to superintend the library, and also the adoption of a rule expressly prohibiting the use of any volume belonging to the library as a text-book in the classes of either institution. The use of the library apartment, too, as a lecture room, interferes much with the due care and safety of the books and furniture. Both that room and the chapel are at present occupied as lecture rooms. . . .(1842:124)

The synod then resolved that a librarian be appointed with reasonable compensation and that General Synod share the cost with the Board of Trustees (1842:127).

Professor Hodenpyl of the Department of Modern Languages was appointed librarian and was requested to prepare a system which would assure preservation of the collection. Nothing was done for the next two years other than the expression of a need for rules regarding the use of the library. It is interesting to note the dependence of the school upon General Synod even so far as to request this body to prepare the rules governing library usage (1843:246).

By checking the holdings against the catalog and acquisition lists, Hodenpyl discovered that many volumes were missing and lamented that "many students have left the seminary, and are now ministers in different places, who have books charged against them" (1844:358). Hodenpyl had written to these ministers regarding the return of these volumes, but the majority of his letters remained unanswered.

With this problem raised before synod, it was time now to take a long look at the purpose and needs of the library. The Board of Superintendents of the seminary was beginning to see clearly the role of the library and sought to have General Synod see this as well. In 1844 they reported that:

> It is the belief of the Board of Superintendents that, by far, too little importance has, in times past, been attached to the library of the college, and to its preservation and increase, and that in consequence of this inattention, many, and some of them very valuable books, have been lost: some it is feared irrecoverable. They would earnestly call the attention of General Synod to this subject, and would express their hope that prompt and effectual measures may be devised not only for the preservation, but for the increase of the library. (1844:358)

At this point in time a rising interest in scholarship was appearing in the Reformed Church (as will be seen below in the compilation of the Amsterdam Correspondence and the denomination's Archives). General Synod was broadening its awareness of the importance of a library and beginning to recognize the intellectual achievements being made by many of its ministers. Two statements of the synod indicate this attitude. The synod's response to the president's statement in 1844 was:

> Your committee concurs in the sentiments expressed in the report relating to the preservation and increase of the college library; for what is a literary or theological institution without a library, or in the possession of a scanty and defective one? But in view of your committee there seems to be no necessity for legislating further in regard to this matter. The committee appointed at the last meeting of General Synod is competent to do all that is required. Let them revive the rules which have become obsolete, add others which are needful, and let these rules be rigidly and impartially enforced by the librarian, sustained by the faculties of both institutions, and no doubt the desired results will be gradually attained. Energy, system, and

perseverance will herein, as in all other desirable objects, triumph over all obstacles. (1844:370)

Synod was reluctant to be involved in the general administration of the library. A few years later they affirmed their desire for a substantial library at New Brunswick by stating:

> A good and well-kept library is so exceedingly important to every literary institution and theological school, that great solicitude is felt by the Faculty, and fully appreciated by your committee, as necessary to all seminaries of learning, for the improvement and attraction of students, for books of the institution.
>
> One chief cause of the great celebrity of the Universities of Germany, the immense concourse of students from all parts of Europe and America, is found in their libraries, containing vast collections of books, easily accessible to students and literary men. Your committee would therefore recommend the necessary appropriation to carry out their own resolution not only, but also a liberal appropriation to increase the library in systematic, historic works, commentaries, and other books. (1847:185)

It would seem that reports of the work of the denomination's scholars in Dutch archives and in European schools were starting to awaken General Synod's interest in scholarship. Both the school and the synod recognized the importance of the adequate care and housing of the collection. In 1847 Van Nest Hall was erected on Rutgers's campus and arrangements were made to have the library moved into better accommodations. Since the safekeeping of the library was now recognized as being of greatest importance, General Synod willingly paid the expenses (1847:184).

With the popularity of the library on the increase, it was clear that this was the time for making further requests of the synod. Therefore, the president of the college reported that many of the volumes were deteriorating and no provision had been made for their repair. "This, as well as the library's enlargement, deserves immediate attention" (1845:482). The synod looked into the matter and authorized rebinding and the preparation and printing of a catalog of the books. This catalog was for the use of the church and the expense would be borne by the General Synod (1845:492). It is easy to see how events led up to that declaration of support for the library in 1847.

Synod was now moving to make the library a first class library. The church was in a period of strength, and interest in scholarly pursuits was at a peak. The collection was now numbering approximately 7,000 volumes with many in Latin and Dutch. In 1852, about 250 volumes of theological works in Dutch were donated by Rensselaer Westerlo from his father's library. The Reverend Dr. Eilardus Westerlo was the brother-in-law of John Livingston. He was educated in the Netherlands and had a number of eighteenth-century theological works. Another catalog was published in 1855 and was the last one of the combined college and seminary library.

The seminary was encountering financial difficulties again, but this time the problem was with the students. The expenses of living in New Brunswick were increasing and the students were going into debt in order to survive. Some were beginning to leave the school in order to study at less expensive institutions. For this reason, the faculty and the board felt a need for a new building which would provide living quarters for the students. A proposal was made by the students to the faculty and was passed on to the board and then to the synod. The request was for a hall which would include dormitories, a refectory, library, lecture rooms, a chapel, and a residence for a professor.

Such a move would necessitate the separation of the existing library between the two schools. In 1855 the synod did not see such a move as very practical and maintained that, "books have been given, the donors of which intended that they should be alike for the benefit of the College and Seminary—given to the library, as it now exists, a bond of union between the two institutions" (1855:597). Thus, the library was now seen as playing an integral role in the literary and theological institution. Indeed, in light of the past problems in raising funds for the library for nearly fifty years, and in light of the recent statements of synod regarding the value of the library, it is likely that synod was wary of two separate institutions requesting funds for development and refurbishing every year.

The synod did agree with the idea of a separate hall for classes since Rutgers was overcrowded at this time and friction was developing between the two schools. Several lots of land were donated to the seminary and a contribution of $30,000 from Mrs. Ann Hertzog enabled the erection of the Peter Hertzog Theological Hall. The hall was dedicated in 1856 and the seminary began to operate in its own facility.

Since a room was provided as a library in the new building which
offered better facilities for the care of the collection, it was obvious
that some action must be taken to place the theological collection in
this building and make it more accessible to the students. The
Reverends Dr. Van Vranken, Campbell, Ludlow, and De Witt were
appointed a committee by General Synod to "act in concert with a
corresponding committee to be appointed by the Trustees of Rutgers
College, to effect an amicable and equitable division of the books in
the Library of the College at New Brunswick" (1857:213). It was
understood that the libraries of both institutions were to remain
accessible to the students of both institutions.

By June 1859 the division was complete. More that 2,000 volumes
were removed from the college library and transferred to Hertzog
Hall. The Board of Superintendents reported that, "we now have in
the theological library upwards of 4,000 volumes; still it is altogether
inadequate to the wants of the institution" (1859:376). The largest
portion of the library was De Witt's collection and this made up the
nucleus of the Hertzog Hall library. The press for funds and
donations of books was once again undertaken as in the early part
of the century. However, this time the church was in a better frame
of mind for this appeal.

In 1862 the library received a large portion of Reverend Van
Vranken's library. Samuel A. Van Vranken had been professor of
didactic theology at the seminary, and professor of the evidences of
the Christian religion and logic at Rutgers from 1841 to 1861. His
library of about 580 volumes represented a significant increase. In
the same year, Reverend George W. Bethune left 1,700 volumes to
the Hertzog Library. John Charles Van Dyke remarks of this man:

> Dr. Bethune was not only a scholar but very much a
> bibliophile and during his years abroad he had collected a
> remarkable number of rare editions from the presses of
> Aldus, Koeberger, Froben, Elzevir, Stevens, Baskerville. . .
> He had a rare appreciation of fine printing and an
> extraordinary gift for picking up the right volume at the
> right time. As a book collector he was a success.[5]

Dr. Bethune was one of the leading ministers in the early-
nineteenth-century church. His own literary output exceeded thirty-
five volumes and pamphlets. He had written several books on
fishing, and tradition has it that his personal library included about
2,000 volumes on the subject. Van Dyke later lamented the fact that

the library did not have these volumes in its collection. A few years later, in 1870, his widow left another 1,170 volumes, and several further bequests drifted in which made a total donation of about 3,000 volumes (1870:13).

The seminary library was now on the path to becoming a major theological research center. One final step remained. The need for a larger building to be used solely for the library was recognized and a site was proposed for a new building east of Hertzog Hall.

The Sage Library

In 1870, Colonel Gardner A. Sage, who had previously donated funds to the seminary, promised to build a library. His contributions to the building, the purchase of books, endowments for maintenance, support of the library in general, a professorship of Old Testament, and scholarships totaled nearly $200,000 over a period of about fifteen years. More than half of this money was designated for the library which bears his name.

The cornerstone of the Sage Library was laid in 1873, and the building was dedicated in 1875. By 1878, nearly $55,000 had been collected for the purchase of books for the new library. The synod appointed a committee consisting of the Reverends T. W. Chambers, C. D. Hartranft, and E. T. Corwin for the selection of books (1875:203). This committee met monthly for eight years and spent the full amount. This committee sought as its criteria to get the best books on every subject regardless of their point of view or language. Their vision of a theological library was one of a well-equipped working library for anyone in the church who had need of it. In their view theology did not take place in a vacuum. They believed that ministers needed to be conversant with broad spectrums of world literature and the sciences. "It was fully recognized at the start that one branch of knowledge cannot be advantageously studied without many cross references to entirely different branches of knowledge, and for that purpose it was thought best to make the library strong in all branches."[6]

The architectural style of the Sage Library is that of a fourth-century Roman basilica. The building represents the nave of a chapel with seven book alcoves on each side representing seven little chapels, which is repeated again in the second story. Each of the alcoves has a stimulating stained glass window which was donated as part of a fund-raising effort. Above these are clerestory windows with an arched ceiling open from the first floor. The present building has an addition which was built in 1929. Intended to maintain the architectural integrity of the building, the Wessel's addition made the library into the shape of a cross. A transept was pushed out on the right and the left and an octagon apse was added at the rear (Van Pelt Memorial Alcove). This gave the building the cross form of the early medieval and Gothic churches. [7]

A portrait gallery was made along the second floor walkway. The paintings were added by John Charles Van Dyke.

The Sage Library now entered what may be called the "golden age" of the theological library. An excellent collection had been developed and sufficient funds were provided for an endowment. John C. Van Dyke entered the service of Sage as assistant librarian in 1878. In 1886 he became the librarian and remained at Sage his entire life. Dr. Van Dyke developed Sage into the excellent research facility that it is today. He developed the library into a scholarly research center which includes a fine collection of encyclopedias, including the famous Diderot in thirty-five folios with the plates; the great folios of ecclesiastic history including Labbeus et Cassartius, the Papal Bulls, the Magdeburg Centuries; the Migne edition of Greek and Latin Fathers in 381 volumes; and an excellent collection of Dutch works which gave it the distinction of having the finest Dutch collection in the country.

The steady growth of Sage is illustrated by the following table:

year	volumes
1873	15,000
1875	20,000
1877	25,000
1879	30,000
1881	32,000
1882	34,000
1884	36,000
1887	38,000
1888	40,000 & 7,000 pamphlets
1893	42,000
1906	47,000 & 9,000 pamphlets [8]

Sage was developed by Van Dyke, who was another of those extraordinary men who appear in the right place at the right time. He greatly determined the collecting policy and brought Sage to public notice. Van Dyke felt that the modern theological library must show the world, "better than any statistics, the growth of the

Church and rank of scholarship now required of those who would be her ministers."[9]

Van Dyke served as librarian for over fifty years until his death in 1932. He was author of more than thirty volumes and influenced the many students who studied at the seminary with his love for scholarship. President Demarest of Rutgers recalls that Sage was Van Dyke's home and his life's work:

> He so largely made that rare library what it is. He knew it all with uncanny completeness. He guided students to the books they wanted or the books he knew they needed and opened to them the ways of intellectual life and stirred the minds of the sensitive to eagerness and new adventure.[10]

The history of Sage Library under Van Dyke and his successors is a great story that deserves separate attention. For our purpose, however, we now turn to the third part of this paper which regards the establishment of the Archives of the Reformed Church in America. Substantial space is provided in the Sage Library for the Archives of the Reformed Church in America. This collection of denominational records greatly adds to the scholarly resources available within the library.

Archives of the Reformed Church in America

A concern for the preservation of the important documents of the Reformed Church in America can be traced back at least two centuries in this country. Included in the 1748 rules of order for the coetus was the provision for the maintenance and preservation of a record book of minutes and correspondence. When the church achieved its independence from the Classis of Amsterdam, this record keeping became the responsibility of the stated clerk of the General Synod. In 1792, the synod resolved to "gather together into one place the papers and record books of the coetus and other early church bodies, as well as accounts of the organization of congregations" (1792:241), so that they might all be preserved in the archives of the church. The concern for preservation of documents was a natural concern for the Dutch Church. The Netherlands had a long tradition for state and church archival preservation.

During the years that followed, inquiry was made from time to time about the location of the General Synod records and about the means of their preservation and protection. While the importance of adequate documentation was never questioned, no extensive effort was made to insure the archives' proper housing. A trunk was used for many years to hold the papers of the General Synod (1814:55). This trunk can still be seen in the Archives.

In 1841, the General Synod asked the Reverend Thomas De Witt to prepare a history of the Reformed Dutch Church which would reach back to its roots in the Netherlands. De Witt reported to synod that, despite the resolution of 1792, nothing seemed to have been brought into the archives. Many valuable and irreplaceable documents had been given into the hands of individual ministers and were subsequently either lost or destroyed. (Hodenpyl had the same regret when he reported on missing volumes in the library.) In the hope of receiving materials relating to the history of the church, De Witt wrote to many ministers and laypeople, asking them to examine whatever consistory minutes or other church records they might have in their possession. He hoped that such a survey would help gather the needed records together so that he could write a comprehensive history. The response was poor, however, and he gave up the idea (1843:271).

This effort did touch off a minor interest in the 1840s in the archives of the church, so arrangements were made for the safe housing of materials in the North Church of New York City, located then at 103 Fulton Street (1845:518). This arrangement proved to be satisfactory for several years, and no mention of the archives occurs again in the minutes of synod until 1861. In 1860 the storehouse of the treasurer of the Board of Direction caught fire and burned, resulting in the loss of important papers. Once again interest was aroused in archival preservation and resulted in the appointment of a committee to look into the question. This committee was charged to "suggest a plan for the collection and preservation of documents relating to the past history of the church" (1866:112).

They performed their task well, housing the archives in a double fire-proof room in the Gardner A. Sage Library. This room was specially prepared for the archives by Mr. Sage (1875:369). The records were transferred but it was apparent that the lack of proper care and preservation had taken a toll on the materials for want of an adequate facility and program. Many documents, undated and unidentified, were mixed in with a jumble of papers having no apparent order; many papers were missing and assumed to have been destroyed. The committee responsible for the care of these papers made an effort to arrange them and then extended an offer to other church judicatories and congregations to deposit their records in this vault for safekeeping. This offer was regularly repeated at the synod and was regularly taken advantage of by churches and agencies.

During the 1840s when the synod asked De Witt to prepare a history of the church, interest was running high in the collection of historical manuscripts. De Witt notified synod of J. Romeyn Brodhead's research, which uncovered many valuable documents relating to the church in archives in the Netherlands. De Witt secured for the denomination's archives the originals of the correspondence from the church in the colonies to the Classis of Amsterdam. Brodhead used these documents in preparing his documentary history of New York and they remained in his and De Witt's custody for nearly thirty years.

The Reverend E. T. Corwin, who was the most significant and prolific historian in the Reformed Church, acquired these and other Netherlands documents. He eventually translated the remainder and published them in a seven-volume set, entitled *T h e Ecclesiastical Records of the State of New York*.[11]

The archives remained at the New Brunswick location and received little attention from the church for the next half century. In the course of his research and writing, Corwin made a remarkable effort to gather the records of the church and contributed many published volumes as the nucleus of what would be the "Dutch Church Room" in Sage. Since there was no one available to work on the proper arrangement and preservation of this material it did not become organized for many years.

In 1928 the Committee on History and Research was established and was appointed custodian of the accumulated materials. It saw to the proper arrangement and description of the archives, providing files and shelving for their general storage and maintenance. This committee was named the official custodian of the Archives in 1955. This committee was later renamed the Commission on History. In 1978, the committee recommended the establishment of a full-time archival program and received approval for this from General Synod.

Today the Archives includes more than 700 linear feet of documents with manuscripts dating to the middle of the seventeenth century. Included in the collection is the Protocol of Henricus Selyns, pastor of the Brooklyn churches in the 1660s, which may be the oldest church record book in New York. The Archives also include correspondence with foreign missionaries and contain a

large collection relating to Japan beginning in 1859. In addition, the
Archives house the record books of many congregations and church
agencies for the last three centuries. Along with the manuscript and
rare book collections of Sage, plus the holdings of the Dutch
Church Room, New Brunswick Theological Seminary houses the
finest collection in the United States relating to the Dutch in early
America.

Conclusion

It can be seen that both the library and the Archives went
through similar periods of frustration and delayed growth. For both
institutions the period of the 1840s offered a "renaissance" within
the church through an increased interest both in scholarship and in
the collection and preservation of those materials which make
scholarship possible. From that period to the present, the library has
been continuing its growth as a research institution.

John Beardslee has served both as archivist for the Reformed
Church in America and as acting librarian at Sage Library. His
dedication to helping others grow into the future out of their
knowledge of the past has been cherished by those fortunate to study
under him or to work with him as a colleague. His love for Sage
Library has been demonstrated during his teaching career at New
Brunswick. John stands solidly in the tradition of those individuals
whose passion for scholarship and love of learning developed the
collection at Sage and enabled the church to recapture its
documentary past through the establishment of a denominational
archives.

VI

From Calvin to Van Raalte:
The Rise and Development of the Reformed Tradition in the Netherlands, 1560-1900

Elton J. Bruins

This essay is an attempt to answer two contemporary questions: Who are we, and where have we come from? The "we" particularly applies to two denominations, the Christian Reformed Church and the Reformed Church in America, and to the educational institutions they nurture: Calvin College and Seminary, Central College, Dordt College, Hope College, Northwestern College, Reformed Bible College, Trinity Christian College, New Brunswick Theological Seminary, and Western Theological Seminary. These institutions and the many congregations of these two denominations stand in the Reformed tradition; that is, they are heirs of the great Protestant reformer, John Calvin. More than that, they are heirs of the Dutch Calvinist movement in particular. The members of the Christian Reformed Church, the Reformed Church in America, as well as the students, faculty, and friends of these educational institutions, can better understand themselves if they understand their heritage grounded in John Calvin and developed through a long history in the Netherlands.

It is our task to answer several questions: Why did the Dutch come to Michigan and Iowa in the mid-nineteenth century? Who were their leaders? Why was there a division in the Dutch Reformed Church in Holland in 1834? Who were key leaders in the old Dutch Church? Why is the Synod of Dort important? How was the Dutch Church in America affected by events in the Netherlands? How did the Reformed Church get started in the Netherlands, and what does all this have to do with Calvin? By asking these questions, we have worked our way to events that took place over 400 years ago, for the answers to these questions begin with John Calvin (1509-64), the theologian of Geneva, Switzerland.

Calvin's career as a reformer has many brilliant facets, but we need emphasize only the two particularly important to the development of the Reformed faith in the Netherlands. Calvin's greatest importance as a reformer came from his writings: commentaries on books of the Bible; correspondence with a host of friends, students, and church leaders throughout Europe; and cogent theological treatises. The best-known and most-valued of these theological writings is the *Institutes of the Christian Religion*, first published in 1536, which went through four enlargements and editions, the final one in 1559.

The second important aspect of Calvin's life was his organizational ability. Not only was he a theologian and an academic, large tasks in themselves, but also a churchman and organizer. Through his work in various capacities, the city of Geneva became, in the words of John Knox, "the most perfect school of Christ ever was on earth since the days of the apostles."[1] Refugees from France and the Netherlands came to Geneva for help and counsel from Calvin; ministers and students came for an education after the University of Geneva was founded in 1559. Through Calvin, Geneva thus became the beacon light of the Swiss Reformation, and its brilliance reached the Netherlands quickly and effectively.

Historians commonly agree that Calvinism developed in the Netherlands because a prior movement, the Brethren of the Common Life (founded by Gerard Groote in 1378),[2] had prepared the soil for the Reformation.[3] Reacting against the seamy side of the medieval church, Groote had attempted to correct abuses and raise the level of Christian life and practice in the Netherlands. He encouraged better education for the clergy and established communal organizations for both men and women in which the simple spiritual life and manual labor were emphasized. The Brethren were allowed to exhort and instruct, but not to preach. They established some fine schools for youths, in one of which the great Erasmus received much of his training. *The Imitation of Christ*, the classic devotional edited by Thomas à Kempis, is a product of the "Devotio Moderna" movement as it was called. The Brethren also copied books and, in general, made a significant contribution to the spiritual lives of many Netherlanders in the fifteenth century.

In fact, the Brethren prepared the Netherlands for the Reformation in general. Soon after 1517, when Luther nailed his theses to the church door at Wittenberg, his writings began to circulate. By the time of his death in 1546, his doctrines as well as those of Zwingli (Zurich) and Martin Bucer (Strasbourg) had spread all over Europe, including the Netherlands.[4] Calvinism was also preceded in the Netherlands by the Anabaptist movement which a Dutchman, Menno Simons, had promoted vigorously among his fellow countrymen. But neither the Lutheran movement nor the Anabaptist movement was destined to lead the Reformation in the Netherlands.

The first Calvinist who made a significant impact in the Netherlands was John à Lasco (1499-1560) who in 1542 was appointed superintendent of the churches of East Friesland in Emden. Under à Lasco's direction, the "mother" church of Holland was created.[5] East Friesland was not a part of the Hapsburg Netherlands and, therefore, lay outside the area where Protestants were being persecuted. Seeking safety, many Dutchmen came to East Friesland where they formed congregations "under the cross." À Lasco organized these congregations according to the Genevan model of Calvin; he also introduced the consistory and the classis and produced a catechism. People trained in these congregations outside the Netherlands were responsible for the organization of Reformed churches in the Netherlands when the Spanish-Hapsburg government collapsed in 1579.

Another key reason for the introduction of Calvinism in the Lowlands was the "Belgic Confession" written by Guido de Bres in 1559. This important confession of faith became so influential that de Bres was executed as a rebel in 1567 for having written it. When the Dutch Reformed synods began to function, at first outside the Netherlands, they immediately adopted the Belgic Confession as a doctrinal statement. When the Provincial Synod of Dort met in 1574, all ministers and school teachers were directed to sign the confession and thus show allegiance to the Reformed faith.[6]

Although the Belgic Confession is still a key confessional statement for the Christian Reformed Church and the Reformed Church in America, it has been overshadowed in popularity by the Heidelberg Catechism. This document was especially influential in bringing Calvinism to Holland. It came via the Rhenish Palatinate which (due to the policy of the Elector Frederick III who began his reign in 1559) was the only Calvinist state in Germany from 1555 to 1618.[7] Frederick was disgusted with the wrangling of the Lutheran

theologians and invited Calvinists to come in their place, a decision
which proved very auspicious for Calvinism, first in Germany and
then in the Netherlands.

Two promising young theologians invited by the elector were
Zacharias Ursinus and Caspar Olevianus. The noted theologian in
Strasbourg, Peter Martyr Vermigli, had been invited in 1561 but
declined the invitation, recommending his brilliant pupil Ursinus,
who arrived in Heidelberg in the fall of 1561.[8] Ursinus had been an
apt pupil not only of the learned Vermigli but also of the master
himself, John Calvin. With the coming of Ursinus and others, the
elector "built a minor provincial university . . . into the most
renowned Calvinist seat of learning of the era. Students and
professors came from every land where Calvinism struck roots,
especially from France, the Netherlands, Italy, and Poland. The
pride of the University was the theology faculty."[9]

The elector put his theologians to work, and a committee headed
by Ursinus and Olevianus produced a catechism which was adopted
by a synod convened at Heidelberg in January 1563. The new
catechism went through four editions in that year alone. Its
acceptance was immediate and widespread, and the Dutch synods
approved of the Heidelberg Catechism as well as the Belgic
Confession. Peter Dathenus, the famous Reformed psalmist,
translated the catechism into Dutch the year it appeared.

Young men still in their twenties when the catechism was
written, Ursinus and Olevianus must have been pleased with the
wide acceptance of their work. Their disappointment, however, was
that Calvin gave them no indication that he approved of the
catechism even though the young men were convinced that they
had produced a work in full accordance with his theology. In fact,
the theologian of Geneva never responded to the young authors who
yearned for his approval.[10] But there was no doubt about the
popularity of the catechism in the Netherlands, for the catechism
has been proclaimed "the only book of instruction in church,
school, and the family" throughout the Netherlands during the
seventeenth century.[11] If this is true, we can assume that the early
Dutch Reformed Church ministers brought the book with them
when they established the Reformed Church in America on
Manhattan Island in 1628. We know with certainty that in 1767 the
Collegiate consistory of New York commissioned a committee
under Dr. Archibald Laidlie to produce an English translation of the
catechism for the Dutch Church in New York.[12]

As powerful and influential as the Belgic Confession and the Heidelberg Catechism were in bringing Calvinism to the Netherlands, and as significant as was the effort of à Lasco in adapting Calvin's organizing genius for Dutch Reformed Christians, political factors may ultimately have determined the spread of Calvinism in the Netherlands and the establishment of the national Dutch Reformed Church. If the Spaniards had not been in control of the Netherlands during the crucial years of the 1560s and 1570s, the future of Calvinism in the Netherlands might have been quite different. By 1566, the nobility and refugees who were determined to end Spanish rule adopted Calvinism. William, Prince of Orange, became the key spokesman of the revolt and a Calvinist. By reason of patriotism, all Netherlanders were induced to become Calvinists to battle the hated Catholic Spaniards.[13]

The Calvinist political revolt surfaced with fierceness in 1566. A wave of image-breaking engulfed the entire country when patriots swept through the churches and smashed all symbols and ornaments that reminded them of the Catholic faith.[14] This event shook the country and its government and led to an "Accord" with Margaret of Parma, Phillip II's regent in the Netherlands, but the war was on with a vengeance. The Duke of Alva pressed the Inquisition into action and created all kinds of devastation. By 1575, Alva was defeated, and the Calvinist minority had won the day in the country of the dikes.

Pieter Geyl, the great secular historian of the Dutch, had to admit: "This phenomenon becomes intelligible only through the state of war, a condition under which detestation of the enemy can cause a society to submit to harsh but purposeful leadership against its real inclinations."[15] As difficult as Geyl found it to believe, the Dutch chose Calvinism and the Reformed faith as their national religion because the Calvinistic Prince of Orange and the other leaders of the country led the country to political freedom. If we understand this, we understand why the Lutherans and Anabaptists who had come to the Netherlands much earlier than the Calvinists had not become the prominent Protestant faith. This history, of course, also tells us why for centuries Roman Catholicism was not a favorite faith of the Netherlands.

The next question that faces us is how Calvinism fared in the Netherlands after the Reformed faith and the Reformed Church had been established. The answer is found by making a quick survey of the two centuries between 1600 and 1800. When the seventeenth century opened, the Dutch Reformed Church was fully established as the national privileged church: the state paid the salaries of the pastors; the three major universities of Leiden, Utrecht, and Amsterdam included faculties of theology which trained all the pastors of the churches; the Mennonite, Lutheran, and Roman Catholic churches had only second-class status but were tolerated to a greater or lesser degree. The national government decided when synods were to be held and even determined when a major translation of the Bible was to be made. All this is quite contrary to the American experience, but what took place in the Netherlands was true for all European Christendom well into the nineteenth century. Thus, when a controversy broke about 1600 between Jacobus Arminius, a moderate Calvinist, and Francis Gomarus, a strict Calvinist, the state was soon involved. The stakes were high, and the loser, in this case John Oldenbarnevelt, a Gomarist but an opponent of Prince Maurice, was beheaded by the state after the Synod of Dort. Political factors, of course, had entered the picture just as at the time of the revolt in 1566.

Jacobus Arminius (1560-1609) was the key theological figure around whom a controversy began to circle. He studied in Geneva under Calvin's successor, Theodore Beza, and in 1588 became a pastor of the Reformed Church in Amsterdam. Arminius was a Calvinist, a surprising fact to many Calvinists today. He read Calvin's commentaries and recommended them as among the finest to be consulted. But Arminius, a moderate Calvinist in comparison with his teacher Beza, was soon placed in a bad light by Francis Gomarus (1563-1645), professor of theology at Leiden University. After 1603, Arminius and Gomarus were colleagues at Leiden and shared equally in teaching future Dutch Reformed pastors Reformed theology. But Gomarus, a follower of Beza, soon came to question Arminius's doctrine of predestination. Like Beza, Gomarus was a supralapsarian who believed that before man and woman fell into sin in the Garden of Eden, God already decreed who among the descendants of Adam and Eve were to be saved and who were to be damned. Calvin never adopted this position but had declared the doctrine of the double decree: since God had elected some people to life eternal with him, he must also have condemned others to eternal damnation. Calvin himself called this the "horrible" decree but nonetheless maintained it as a theological truth. For Calvin, the doctrine of predestination was not just a truth for the Christian's comfort; he maintained that God truly would call out a people for salvation in Christ and not allow evil and Satan to have the last word.

A Reformed pastor and teacher, Arminius could not agree with the extreme views of Beza and Gomarus. However, Arminius considered himself truly Reformed, Calvinist, and biblical in the position he took. Arminius taught the New Testament paradox that God would have all people to be saved and come to a knowledge of the truth, that God takes the initiative in mankind's salvation process, and that the response of faith which a person is invited to make is a response to God's gracious call. In answer to the accusations and challenges made against him by Gomarus, Arminius said: "The act of believing is a choice of free will which has been brought from its addiction to evil to a point of flexibility by grace."[16] Arminius was convinced that no one could personally believe the Christian message without the prior grace of God at work in his or her heart, but wanted to bring out the New Testament emphasis that the person touched by God's hand has the privilege and responsibility to respond to God's gracious call.

In another statement, Arminius tried to state the doctrine of predestination in such a way that God's foreknowledge could be taken seriously. That is to say, his position was that God does take into consideration mankind's response to the invitation of grace. Arminius said: "By an absolute predestination God wills to save individuals whom he foresees as believing and persevering and to damn those whom he foresees as not believing."[17] In this statement, Arminius is simply trying to echo the paradox the New Testament teaches on this crucial doctrine. He was convinced that his views agreed with the Belgic Confession and the Heidelberg Catechism and stated as much.

Americans in the Reformed tradition who read these Calvinistic statements of Arminius may well be perplexed by this time. Calvin's thoughts and what is often called Calvinism can be radically different. On the American scene, Arminianism is the idea that divine grace is not a prerequisite for mankind's cooperating with and sharing in the salvation process. Billy Graham, one of the most popular Arminians of our day, can be quoted as saying that if you will, you can believe. Human responsibility to believe is stressed in place of the idea that God initiates grace in the salvation process. On the contrary, Arminius said that "cooperation is not the means to renewal; it is the result of renewal."[18]

The extreme Calvinists won the day. Arminius took sick during the controversy and died in 1609. Nonetheless, his followers pursued his thought and published "The Remonstrance of 1610." From that title came the name given to his followers: Remonstrants. The followers of Gomarus were called Counter Remonstrants, and to settle the battle between them a national synod was called into session during 1618-19. That synod, the Synod of Dort, went down in history as a major turning point in Dutch Calvinism. It was the first national synod that the government called; not only did clergymen and elders attend, but six deputies represented the government, or the States-General as it was called. Twenty-seven delegates came from other countries and, therefore, the session had to be conducted in Latin. Johannes Bogerman was the presiding officer, and Simon Episcopius led the Remonstrant delegation. The sixteen clergymen in his group were treated as second-class citizens and not officially seated. Their doctrines were condemned by the synod, and the clergymen were threatened with exile if they preached their beliefs.

The conclusions of the Synod of Dort were published as canons under five heads, summarized in this way by John T. McNeill:

(1) election is founded on God's purpose;

(2) the efficacy of Christ's atonement extends to the elect only;

(3) the Fall has left man in a state of corruption and helplessness;

(4) regeneration is an inward renewal of the soul and will and is wholly a work of God; and

(5) God so preserves the elect, ever renewing their repentance, patience, humility, gratitude, and good works, that, despite their sins, they do not finally fall away from grace.[19]

These are the so-called five points of Calvinism as understood by the Dortian fathers and are better remembered by the mnemonic device T U L I P: total depravity, unconditional election, limited atonement, irresistible grace, and perseverance of the saints. The Canons of Dort, which along with the Belgic Confession and the Heidelberg Catechism were adopted by the Dutch Reformed Church, have become the "standards of unity" of the daughter churches in America which have continued their allegiances to these three major confessional statements of sixteenth- and seventeenth-century Reformed Calvinism.

In a major way, the Synod of Dort set up the pattern of life for the Dutch Reformed Church and Dutch Calvinism until the Napoleonic takeover of the Netherlands in 1795. But a few things need to be said to give some understanding of the post-Dortian period. The church life of these two centuries centered primarily on Johannes Coccejus (1603-69) and Gisbertus Voetius (1589-1676), theologians and writers who came to represent two major schools of thought.

Coccejus was professor of theology at Leiden University; Voetius held the same position at Utrecht. Voetius, a delegate at the Synod of Dort, was an uncompromising foe of Arminius. Coccejus became known for the development of covenantal theology and worked at length on his explanation of the covenant of works and the covenant of grace. Since the Latin word for covenant is *foedus*, his theology was called "federal theology." Coccejus accepted the philosophy of René Descartes and introduced his thought into Dutch theology; Voetius adamantly opposed this development and criticized Coccejus severely. The two men became bitter opponents, and they and their followers waged a constant theological war. For years "Coccejans" were in control at Leiden while the "Voetians" had their sphere of influence at Utrecht.

Despite the personal and theological differences between Coccejus and Voetius, they did have one thing in common: both were Scholastic theologians, holding that the medieval understanding of Aristotle was as vital to their theological systems as St. Thomas Aquinas was to Roman Catholic theology. In this way, they differed greatly from Calvin who had not used any philosophical base for his theology except a mild Platonism.[20] In fact, both Calvin and Luther despised medieval Scholasticism which emphasized deductive and syllogistic reasoning. Calvin was a keen thinker, but for him reason was not on the same level as faith as it was in Catholic and Protestant Scholasticism. Calvin's thinking tried to keep biblical categories uppermost, but Scholastics such as Coccejus and Voetius were interested in metaphysical matters and speculative thought, particularly in reference to the doctrine of God.[21] Even Ursinus who wrote the catechism showed signs of an incipient Protestant Scholasticism in the commentary he wrote to explain the catechism.

The Reformed Church in America was influenced directly by both Coccejus and Voetius. Theodorus Jacobus Frelinghuysen who came to serve the Dutch Church in America in 1720 was raised in the "Voetian" school. His severe antagonist, Henricus Boel, pastor of the Collegiate Church in New York, was a Coccejan. Frelinghuysen exemplified the mystical piety that had originated in the Brethren of the Common Life and continued through Voetius, helping to explain why Frelinghuysen insisted upon a particular expression of piety among his parishioners. Frelinghuysen, like Voetius, was a "Precisionist." Voetius wrote: "We define 'precision' as the exact or perfect human action conforming to the law of God as taught by God, and genuinely accepted, intended and desired by believers."[22] Voetian piety precisely determined such things as one's behavior on the Lord's Day, giving for missions, the length of one's hair, and similar small details along the entire spectrum of Christian behavior.

When John Henry Livingston (1746-1825) decided to join the Dutch Reformed Church and get his theological education in the Netherlands, he entered the University of Utrecht (at the age of twenty), already having graduated from Yale College. According to his biographer, Alexander Gunn, he took counsel with respected pastors and theologians in the Netherlands before he decided to enter Utrecht.[23] Gunn's account of Livingston's educational experience in the Netherlands indicates clearly that the Voetian piety was still much in evidence, and all Livingston's expressions of piety seem to come directly from this tradition. Moreover, the textbook for theology he used at Utrecht was the one studied earlier in the eighteenth century by Frelinghuysen: Marck's *Medulla*, the text which remained the basic theological text at the New Brunswick Theological Seminary until well into the nineteenth century. Livingston's influence in the American Dutch Church related directly to his Dutch experience, for in 1792 when the Reformed Church in America became an independent ecclesiastical body he chose the Church Order of Dort as the primary church order. In addition, Livingston wrote the "Explanatory Articles," adapting the Church Order of Dort to the American scene. He also decided to eliminate the "Anathemas" against Arminius's followers which were part of the Canons of the Synod of Dort. It is not at all, therefore, a surprise that the American Dutch Church was influenced by the Dutch theological and ecclesiastical scene since the American congregations were directly under the authority of the Classis of Amsterdam until the ties were broken during the American Revolution.

The next era in the rise and development of Calvinism in the Netherlands began with Napoleon Bonaparte's invasion of Holland in 1795.[24] The stadtholder, Prince William V, fled to England, never to return. When the lowlands regained freedom, the son of the prince became William the First of the Netherlands, which now included Belgium as well as Holland. During this period of radical change, the Dutch Reformed Church was jolted, having been separated from the state in 1796. This action was not protested generally, but the pastors soon paid a price. After 1799, the state no longer paid their salaries. Instead, the parishioners had to raise money for the pastor's salary. But this unusual practice was reversed by the new king, William. He offered to restore a liberal subsidy to the church, and the Dutch Reformed Church "preferred the material advantages of an alliance with the new administration." [25]

King William I also reestablished the state-church relationship. By royal decree of January 7, 1816, he asserted the "Concept of a General Order for the Administration of the Reformed Church in the Kingdom of the Netherlands." Concerned only to have the church properly administered, he convened a synod which met in July 1816. Pastors received back pay, with the father of Albertus C. Van Raalte receiving 570 guilders as back payment on his yearly salary of 224 guilders. Most likely, Van Raalte's father gave thanks that the Netherlands again had a king who honored the Sabbath and brought order to the church. King William also decreed that all Reformed Church clergymen would ascribe to the three Standards of Unity and be orthodox in belief and practice.

But times had changed. For one thing, the Mennonites, who still believed in the separation of church and state, refused to accept the new church constitution and the administration of church affairs by the government. In addition, the thinking of the clergy in many churches had been so affected by the ideas of the Enlightenment that many could simply not return to the old ways. Also, it was at this time that a new movement called the *Reveil* began a rebirth of the old piety in the Dutch Church. The *Reveil* was similar to other movements taking place in Germany and Switzerland and not unlike the revival efforts of the Moravians and Methodists. There was also a renewal of the conventicle system which Voetius had fostered two centuries earlier, and Christians were encouraged to engage in spiritual exercises called *oefeningen*. Members of the *Reveil* were concerned for the renewal of the Dutch Reformed Church but did not intend to leave the church to accomplish that task.

In spite of the intention of the *Reveil* group not to separate from the church, many Dutch Christians felt differently. Theological liberalism had made an impact upon the Dutch Reformed Church in spite of King William's desire for Dortian orthodoxy. The conventicles invariably gave rise to criticism of the Dutch Church. On the other hand, several theologians in the church clearly believed that the Dortian viewpoint had its limitations. In this mixed scene, leadership for a movement to separate from the mother church was exerted by Hendrik de Cock, a pastor at Ulrum, and Hendrick P. Scholte, a recent graduate from Leiden. De Cock's reasons for separation were typical of those of many other reformers who had hoped to change the church but finally chose to leave the Reformed Church because they considered their task hopeless. De Cock had undergone a great personal change after he began reading Calvin's *Institutes*. Having determined that the church no longer was faithful to Dort and its doctrinal position, he intended to lead his people and like-minded Christians "back to Dort."

The separation from the Dutch Church, to which he gave his leadership, is called the Secession of 1834. Once de Cock felt that internal reform of the church was no longer possible he urged his flock and others to follow him into a new church.[26] In his ecclesiastical practices, such as baptizing children of parents from other parishes, he was bound to come into direct conflict with the parent church. His classis suspended him, and his followers came into conflict with the authorities.

Even though the French had lost control of the Netherlands in 1813, the Penal Code of Napoleon had remained in effect, and Articles 291, 292, and 294 were used against the separatists. All new religious groups had to be given permission by the government to form, and severe fines were levied if unauthorized religious meetings, or meetings of more than twenty persons, were held. [27]

But, though the Seceders experienced considerable opposition during the early years of the new church's existence, it grew in spite of the government's efforts. The new movement seemed to catch the attention of those people in Holland who yearned for the old days of Dutch orthodoxy and the old piety that had its roots in the Brethren of the Common Life. The movement picked up new leadership in the persons of four bright young men: Hendrick P. Scholte, Albertus C. Van Raalte, Anthonie Brummelkamp, and Samuel Van Velzen. Van Raalte, Brummelkamp, and Van Velzen had close family ties because each had married a daughter of the De Moen family of Leiden. All these men threw themselves into the work of the Secession and pastored churches. In time, Van Velzen and Brummelkamp became professors in the new theological school established in Kampen. Scholte and Van Raalte led many Seceders to America.

Through Scholte and Van Raalte we have the development of the Seceder Church or Gereformeerde Kerk in Michigan and Iowa. Understanding the theology and piety of these men, we can understand the development of this branch of Calvinism in America. Since both men were so fully engaged in establishing theocratic communities in America,[28] they produced no significant theological writings. But the type of piety they brought from Holland is clearly seen, especially in Van Raalte's life. Van Raalte's piety is much like that of John H. Livingston and distinctly Voetian. But Van Raalte had studied at Leiden, not Utrecht; and the theological faculty at Leiden gave no evidence at all of Voetian piety since followers of Coccejus had long dominated Leiden's theological faculty. But, whatever the source, Van Raalte evidenced the deep piety which had existed for centuries in his homeland.[29]

According to Dr. Gordon Spykman, "his [Van Raalte's] sermons lay a heavy emphasis on inner piety."[30] Van Raalte is also solidly within the context of Dutch Reformed scholasticism; for him, "Calvin was clothed in scholastic garments."[31] But Spykman does not attempt to understand or search out the sources of Van Raalte's piety. Actually, Dr. Spykman tries to make a "Kuyperian" out of Van Raalte, and that is impossible to do.

Van Raalte was not a "Kuyperian," a follower of Abraham Kuyper (1837-1920). The aged Van Raalte could have adopted Kuyper's ideas, but as a young man Van Raalte showed no special interest in the rising, articulated, young theologian who was coming to the fore in the Netherlands during the latter part of the nineteenth century. It is certain that Van Raalte knew Kuyper, even though Van Raalte was in America and Kuyper in Holland, for they corresponded over the question of assisting a young Dutch immigrant who had come to Holland, Michigan. But after his retirement in 1866, Van Raalte did not seem very interested in the Dutch theological scene.

Abraham Kuyper was instrumental in Neo-Calvinism, the revival of Calvinism in Holland during the later part of the nineteenth century. A prolific writer, theologian, and journalist, he soon made his mark. In 1880, he founded the Free University.[32] In 1886, he led out of the old Dutch Reformed Church a movement call *Doleantie* which in 1892 joined with the old De Cock-Scholte Seceder movement of 1834. In 1898, he was invited to come to America to give the Stone Lectures at Princeton Theological Seminary and soon after the turn of the century became the prime minister of the Netherlands. Kuyper was concerned with bringing Calvinism to bear on politics and social life, not just on the personal, inner life of individual Christians.

How does the influence of Van Raalte and Kuyper bear upon the Christian Reformed Church and the Reformed Church in America? In 1850, only four years after his arrival in America, Van Raalte joined the old Dutch Reformed Church in America, believing that it had not suffered the ravages of liberalism that the mother church in the Netherlands had undergone. While the majority of the immigrants Van Raalte had led to Michigan, as well as many other immigrants in Illinois, Iowa, and Wisconsin who agreed with him, followed him into the Reformed Church in America, the few who did not agree led a secession movement of four congregations and formed the Christian Reformed Church. Back in the Netherlands, the Gereformeerde Kerk or Christian Reformed Church (as it was called after 1869) thought at first that the new Christian Reformed secession movement was unnecessary and continued to support Van Raalte and the union of the Classis of Holland with the Reformed Church in America. But in the early 1880s, the Christian Reformed Church of the Netherlands changed its mind about the soundness of the Reformed Church in America because the Reformed Church had not taken a tough stand against Free Masonry. Consequently, the infant Christian Reformed Church in America received the blessing of the Christian Reformed Church in the Netherlands.

Such an action would have been of little significance except that large groups of immigrants from Holland continued to come to America from 1880 until 1923, when uncontrolled immigration was cut off by the United States. Many, if not most, of the Dutch who came after 1880 joined the Christian Reformed Church here, although some joined the Reformed Church in America because Reformed Church congregations in Holland, Michigan, were just as much against Free Masons as were the Dutch Christians. After 1880, the Christian Reformed Church in the United States grew significantly. After 1892 when the *Doleantie* movement of Kuyper joined forces with the Christian Reformed Church in the Netherlands, nearly all Dutch immigrants to the United States felt more at home in the American Christian Reformed Church than in the old Seceder section of the Reformed Church in America.

By 1900 Kuyper's followers, who made up the *Doleantie* movement, infused Neo-Calvinism into the immigrant congregations of the Christian Reformed Church and took strong root in Calvin College and Seminary. Kuyper's ideas also took root in and among the descendants of Van Raalte, especially at Western Theological Seminary. Professors such as Henry E. Dosker and Nicholas Steffens knew Kuyper and corresponded with him regularly.[33] Many students at Western Seminary knew their Kuyper, and Kuyper's works appeared on the bookshelves of Reformed Church pastors as well as those of Christian Reformed pastors.

In conclusion, because Calvin's thought was kept alive by faithful Dutch Christians through a period of four centuries, John Calvin's disciples are very much alive in Western Michigan, in both the Christian Reformed Church and the Reformed Church. A direct line extends from Geneva to Ulrum to Michigan in the descendants of Calvin who continue to believe that the Reformed faith has something of great value to offer people at this time and in the future.

VII
From Pessimism to Optimism: Francis Turretin and Charles Hodge on "The Last Things"

Earl Wm. Kennedy

John Walter Beardslee III wrote a weighty doctoral dissertation in 1957 on the dramatic theological shift at Geneva from the scholastic Reformed orthodoxy of Francis Turretin (1623-87) to the Enlightenment theology of his son, Jean-Alphonse Turretin (1671-1737).[1] My own doctoral work, completed in 1968, centered on the unwitting but significant theological deviations from Francis Turretin disseminated by Charles Hodge (1797-1878), the "Nestor" of Old School Presbyterian theology who taught at Princeton Seminary for over half a century. Hodge sought faithfully to transmit the elder Turretin's orthodox system to latter-day Calvinists in the post-Enlightenment, "evangelical," American religious world of the mid-nineteenth century.[2] The facts that Dr. Beardslee's dissertation sometimes makes reference to Hodge in his comparisons of the two Turretins, and that Hodge, largely through his many students and his three-volume *Systematic Theology* and other writings, has exercised a considerable influence on the theological ethos of the Reformed Church in America, make it appropriate to include a short comparative study of Turretin and Hodge in a volume dedicated to Beardslee.[3] Also, one of the most striking turnabouts—illustrative of the radically different theological worlds of Turretin and Hodge—occurs in Princeton's (and Hodge's) departure from Turretin's eschatological pessimism. This change Beardslee has noted more than once.[4]

In our "apocalyptic" times biblical eschatology and its interpretation throughout church history have received a great deal of attention. The Protestant Reformation spawned considerable "end times" speculation, although Calvin and most of the Reformed (e.g., The Second Helvetic Confession of Heinrich Bullinger) opposed "chiliasm" (the temporal, visible reign of Christ in an earthly paradise) and date-setting. Calvin was hopeful without being naively optimistic. His eschatology provided him with the dynamic for Christian action and obedience in the reordering of society.[5]

Seventeenth-century Calvinism deserted Calvin's views by ranging from activistic post-millennial Puritanism to quietistic amillennialism with little hope for this world.[6] Francis Turretin, who lived late in the century when the outlook for Protestantism looked grim, was possessed of a pious siege mentality which despaired of earthly progress for the earth. His views on the mission of the church and the signs of the times reveal his pessimism.

The particularism of Turretin's theology of the divine decrees extends to his doctrine of God's eternal call to sinners by means of the gospel, over against the "hypothetical universalism" of the French Reformed school of Saumer, which sought to mediate between the theology of the Synod of Dort and that of the Arminians.[7] He affirms the particularity of the covenant of grace in contrast to the universality of the covenant of works. This means that the covenant of grace is made only with those who are elect in Christ, although it may be presented externally to the reprobate.[8] The men of Saumer taught that God's grace is objectively presented to every person in the works of nature and providence, but they did not join the Arminians in advocating a universal, sufficient grace. Against both errors, Turretin maintained the historical Reformed view that neither external calling by the word of the gospel nor internal (effectual) calling by the Holy Spirit is extended by God to all persons, although the former is less narrow than the latter.

Turretin and his theological foes agreed that not all persons actually are saved, that the gospel is not preached everywhere, that no one is saved apart from Christ, and that God gives temporal blessings to everyone. The basic issues between Turretin and the school of Saumer may be stated as follows: 1) whether God designed the covenant of grace for all persons; and 2) whether adults can be saved through knowledge of God derived from nature and providence apart from knowledge of the gospel. Turretin answers both of these questions in the negative.[9]

While some dying infants are elect and may be saved by Christ apart from knowledge of him, while Old Testament believers were saved without a distinct knowledge of Christ, and while there is a theoretical possibility of an extraordinary work of grace in which the Spirit may operate apart from the ordinary means of the Word, Turretin insists that natural theology is wholly inadequate to give a true picture of God as creator and preserver, and especially as redeemer. The general benevolence of God observed in nature, conscience, and history is a completely insufficient representation of his saving mercy in Christ. The Reformed consensus is that

> . . . the theology or true Religion, through which salvation can come to man after the fall, is only one, i.e., that revealed in the Word of the Law and Gospel; and. . . all other religions except this one are either impious and idolatrous, or false and erroneous; which, although retaining some obscure and imperfect notions of the Law and that which may be known of God, yet are of no further use than to render man inexcusable.[10]

Turretin argues on the basis of New Testament passages that "there can be no saving Religion without Christ and faith in him," and that ". . . Christ is revealed no where except in the Gospel; nor is faith given without the Word, since it comes by hearing, Romans 10:17."[11]

Turretin is as positive that countless people have never heard the gospel as he is that the knowledge of Christ is the only way to salvation. The covenant of grace has never been universal, since "...innumerable men and peoples exist at the present day, who are shrouded in the darkness of Paganism, who have never heard anything of Christ and the covenant of grace. . . Romans 10:14."[12] But this fact—vividly impressed upon the seventeenth-century European consciousness by the recent exploring, trading, and colonizing by the maritime powers—does not lead Turretin to urge the fulfillment of the Great Commission. Instead, he appears to fall back upon the doctrine of providence to explain—if not entirely to excuse—the Protestant failure to heed the missionary mandate of Christ.

> Now if God seriously intended their (the heathens) salvation, if he willed to extend to them the covenant of grace, why was he unwilling that it should be revealed to them? and why did he not correct the negligence of men, which he undoubtedly foresaw?[13]

In fairness, however, we should recognize that, humanly speaking, the times were not auspicious for Turretin to be mission-minded. Circumstances were such as to engender discouragement among the Reformed of Geneva and elsewhere. The Protestants of France were a church under the cross and many Huguenot refugees fled to Geneva. The depredations of Louis XIV beyond his own borders were cause for considerable alarm. Furthermore, some of the French Reformed refugees helped disseminate in Geneva itself the bothersome notions of the Saumer professors. One reason Roman Catholic Portugal and Spain were able to promote foreign missions was that they were both early colonial powers. When Protestant nations, such as England and the Netherlands, became major colonial powers in the seventeenth century, missionary interest began to grow there as well. It should not be forgotten that Geneva was landlocked.[14] Thus, judging from appearances, Turretin's pessimism and defensiveness were well-grounded. Instead of the more active, even militant approach of Calvin and the Puritans, Turretin cultivated an inner piety and the hope that Christ would soon return to deliver his people from all their miseries.[15]

He seems convinced that the only way things would be improved was by the Second Advent rather than by a positive presentation of Christ in the covenant of grace to the whole world. There are five general signs which will precede the return of Christ and the end of the world: 1) many false prophets; 2) wars and calamities; 3) great persecution of the faithful; 4) extreme corruption of morals; and 5) the universal preaching of the gospel throughout the whole world. In addition there are two special signs: 1) the revelation of the Antichrist (the Roman Catholic Church); and 2) the conversion of the Jews. Turretin, who was partly Jewish himself, seems to be genuinely concerned that the Jews should acknowledge Jesus as their Messiah, and disappointed with the slowness of their conversion in his own day. He specifically names four (the four signs of evil) of the five general signs as being visible in his day, and declares that, for the most part, the general signs have been fulfilled, as well as the revelation of the Antichrist. The only hopeful and positive general sign, that having to do with the universal preaching of the gospel, is the only one not mentioned as already having happened; it is simply passed over in silence.[16]

Turretin opposes the crasser, heretical chiliasts who anticipate an earthly millennium with sensual pleasures (including many wives and Jewish worship restored in Palestine) as well as the more innocuous millennialism of such seventeenth-century Reformed theologians as Joseph Mede and Johann Heinrich Alsted. This kind of historical hope Turretin simply cannot accept because he believed that the church must suffer, not reign, in this life. Although he refused to set any date for the Second Coming he does seem to encourage the expectation that Christ will return soon. The point is that his concentration on "these sad times in which we live" and "the high waves on which Christ's little boat is tossed" suggests that he is convinced that the only way the situation could be improved was not by a positive presentation of the gospel to all people but by patiently enduring the buffets of the world for the (anticipated) short time remaining before the Second Advent. He interprets the church militant as the church under the cross, passively enduring numberless evils. While the ancient church prayed for the delay of Antichrist, we "in this miserable age and most mournful state of the afflicted church and almost overwhelmed under the weight of trials, ought to cry out with redoubled wishes and breathings, 'Come Lord Jesus, yea, come quickly.'"[17] Thus, as far as Turretin is concerned, external calling is not universal and there seems to be no real expectation that it might become so.

Turretin echoes the Canons of Dort and the Helvetic Consensus Formula in insisting that external calling to all persons promiscuously, is serious and sincere on God's part, but he assumes that this calling takes place primarily, if not exclusively, in the church visible.[18]

Clearly, Turretin is anything but a "positive" thinker. For that we need to turn to the New World, the nineteenth century, and Charles Hodge, who was both a self-professed "optimist" and a conscious follower of the theology of Francis Turretin, whose three-volume *Institutio* was the textbook in dogmatics at Princeton Seminary from its inception in 1812 until Hodge's own three-volume magnum opus (1871-72) replaced it. But in spite of Hodge's desire to be faithful to the system of divinity laid down by Turretin, both his own personality and the nineteenth-century American milieu made it virtually impossible for him to be theological clone of the last of the orthodox Reformed Genevans. The odd thing is that Hodge seems to have been almost totally unaware of his subtle—and not so subtle— departures from Turretin.[19] Among the more obvious deviations is Hodge's postmillennial optimism.

The teachings of Alsted, Mede, and others about a coming earthly millennial glory were popular in the American colonies from the beginning, especially New England.[20] In the Great Awakening Jonathan Edwards revived this belief and tied millennial expectations more firmly to the "new" world. This, coupled with the success of the American Revolution and the establishment of the United States of America (and the concurrent cataclysmic events of the French Revolution and the Napoleonic wars in Europe), brought to birth the American "civil religion." The United States had a God-given role in the "latter days" to inaugurate a "new order of the ages."[21] John Henry Livingston (1746-1825), the "father" of the Reformed Church in America and the first professor at New Brunswick Seminary, was a firm postmillennialist and patriot but tied his hope for the millennium (to begin by A.D. 1999) more to the nascent Protestant foreign missionary enterprise than to American national destiny.[22] Frequently, postmillennial optimism went hand in hand in the nineteenth century with reformist zeal to abolish slavery, war, and other evils, and to bring about a beautiful age of moral, intellectual, and material progress, aided by "science."[23] But during the course of the nineteenth century, especially after the Civil War, premillennialism began to challenge postmillennialism in American Protestantism. The premillennialists had no hope for progress in this world; their program was to evangelize until Jesus returned. There was little reformist sentiment among them. This brought about "the great reversal" in American evangelicalism, in which social involvement was dramatically reduced and more or less left to the "liberals" and their "social gospel."[24] The pessimism of the premillennialists regarding earthly prospects is akin to that of Francis Turretin, although he was not a premillennialist (let alone a dispensationalist) of the modern sort. He was more of a gloomy amillennialist. But what of Charles Hodge's eschatology and attitude toward the world?

Hodge's doctrine of external calling is much the same as Turretin's, except that the call is to be made to the whole world and not merely to the visible church.[25] It is universal in the sense that it is "confined to no age, nation, or class of men."[26] It is

> addressed to all men. The command of Christ to his Church was to preach the gospel to every creature. Not to irrational creatures, and not to fallen angels; these two classes are excluded by the nature and design of the gospel. Further than this there is no limitation, so far as the present state of existence is concerned. We are commanded to make the offer of salvation through Jesus to every human being on the face of the earth. We have no right to exclude any man; and no man has any right to exclude himself.[27]

The contrast with Turretin's myopic vision could hardly be greater. Furthermore, the decrees must be interpreted in the light of the Great Commission, not vice versa: "If . . . any one holds any view of the decrees of God, or of the satisfaction of Christ, or of any other Scriptural doctrine, which hampers him in making this general offer of the gospel, he may be sure that his views or his logical processes are wrong."[28] This universal external call is, however, consistent with the doctrines of predestination and of the sincere offer of the gospel to the reprobate.[29]

Hodge is in substantial agreement with Westminster and Turretin in teaching that for adults salvation is not ordinarily possible without knowledge of Christ. In spite of his extensive use of natural theology, he insists that it is insufficient to lead men to salvation; the heathen are "in a state of fatal ignorance."[30] In extraordinary cases, however, God may directly and supernaturally reveal enough truth to the heathen to bring about their salvation.[31] This is not precisely the doctrine of Turretin, who simply says that the Spirit may operate apart from the Word.

Hodge's reaction to the doctrine that adults cannot ordinarily be saved without knowledge of the gospel is quite the opposite from that of Turretin, who sees no missionary imperative, and who attributes the lack of the universal spread of the gospel to God's providence. "We must not charge the ignorance and consequent perdition of the heathen upon God. The guilt rests on us. We have kept to ourselves the bread of life, and allowed the nations to perish." "The proper effect of the doctrine that the knowledge of the gospel is essential to the salvation of adults, instead of exciting opposition to God's word or providence, is to prompt us to greatly increased exertion to send the gospel to those who are perishing for lack of knowledge."[32] Princeton Seminary and Hodge (as well as New Brunswick and Western seminaries) participated in the general nineteenth-century American evangelical enthusiasm for foreign missions. The seminary sent out scores, including one of Hodge's own sons, to the foreign fields.[33] Hodge's writings and sermons abound in missionary fervor.[34] The 1903 Northern Presbyterian revision of the Westminster Confession reflects the spirit of the times by adding a chapter, "Of the Love of God and Missions."

Missionary enthusiasm and postmillennial optimism go hand in hand in Hodge. In general, he is quite circumspect in matters eschatological,[35] but he waxes dogmatic in championing postmillennialism (he does not use the word) against premillennialism. Hodge is also stronger than Turretin in condemning chiliasm. The reason for this may be partly that premillennialism was more extreme and more popular in Hodge's day, and partly that Turretin and the premillennialists shared a pessimism regarding earthly society unknown to the optimistic Hodge.

There seems to be both more optimism and less expectation of the imminent return of Christ in Hodge than in Turretin. Of the seven signs Turretin gives as preceding the Second Advent, Hodge gives special attention to only three: 1) the universal preaching of the gospel; 2) the conversion of the Jews; and 3) the appearance of the Antichrist.[36] The first two are optimistic signs, and the third is pessimistic, but Hodge interprets the doctrine of the Antichrist largely exegetically and historically, not in terms of the current miseries of the church, as Turretin did. Hodge's Antichrist is something of a paper tiger.[37] He takes pleasure in reporting and endorsing the nearly universal preaching of the gospel. Presumably the conversion of the Jews as a nation will follow the conversion of the Gentiles, but Hodge does not seem very concerned about it.[38] He slights and postpones into the distant future four of the five pessimistic signs which Turretin saw as fulfilled in his own time: false prophets, wars and disasters, persecution of Christians, and moral declension.[39] Hodge makes only scattered allusions to the trials and apostasy through which the church will pass just prior to Christ's return.

In speaking of the wheat and the tares in the kingdom of heaven, he remarks that

> Experience concurs with Scripture in teaching that the kingdom of Christ passes through many vicissitudes; that it has its times of depression and its seasons of exaltation and prosperity. About this in the past, there can be no doubt. Prophecy sheds a sufficiently clear light on the future to teach us, not only that this alternation is to continue to the end, but, more definitely, that before the second coming of Christ there is to be a time of great and long continued prosperity, to be followed by a season of decay and of suffering, so that when the Son of Man comes he shall hardly find faith on the earth.[40]

Hodge's postmillennial optimism comes into sharp focus as he continues:

It is to be hoped, there is to be a period of millenial [sic] glory on earth, and a still more glorious consummation of the Church in heaven. This period is called a millennium because in Revelation it is said to last a thousand years, an expression which is perhaps generally understood literally. Some however think it means a protracted season of indefinite duration . . . Others, assuming that in the prophetic language a day stands for a year, assume that the so-called millennium is to last the hundred and sixty-five thousand years. During this period, be it longer or shorter, the Church is to enjoy a season of peace, purity, and blessedness such as it has never yet experienced.

The principal reason for assuming that the prophets predict a glorious state of the Church prior to the second advent is, that they represent the Church as being thus prosperous and glorious on earth . . . This state is described as one of spiritual prosperity; God will pour out his Spirit upon all flesh; knowledge shall everywhere abound; wars shall cease to the ends of the earth, and there shall be nothing to hurt or destroy in all my holy mountain, saith the Lord. This does not imply that there is to be neither sin nor sorrow in the world during this long period, or that all men are to be true Christians. The tares are to grow together with the wheat until the harvest. The means of grace will still be needed; conversion and sanctification will be then what they ever have been. It is only a higher measure of the good which the Church has experienced in the past that we are taught to anticipate in the future. This however is not the end. After this and after the great apostasy which is to follow, comes the consummation.[41]

Hodge's eschatological timetable may be summarized thus: the gospel is now progressing so well that the millennium cannot be far away; the millennial age will last a long time, during which the church will prosper as never before; after the millennium will come the great apostasy (which Turretin believed to be occurring in his own day); finally, Christ will come back. On this construction, Hodge cannot have seriously expected either any imminent serious trials for the church or an imminent Second Advent.[42] Charles Augustus Briggs, no theological friend of Old Princeton, called attention to the fact that the doctrine of a future millennium does not appear in the Westminster Confession (not to mention Turretin). He complains that this teaching

> is not so innocent as it appears to be on the surface. It changes the faith of the Church in the imminency of the second advent of Christ. It makes the millennium the great hope of the future instead of the presence of the Redeemer Himself. The Messiah is the great hope of the Church . . . But the current theology pushes the Messiah behind the millennium, and fixes the hope of men upon an illusion and a delusion of human conceit and folly.[43]

Nevertheless, Hodge also teaches, as a subordinate motif, that Christ could come soon, that the church should be ready, and that the prosecution of the missionary task will help to "prepare the way of the Lord."[44] The tension between "any moment" and "the signs of the times" is to be found in the New Testament itself, but Hodge's postmillennial optimism may not be so much an induction from the Bible as it is a reflection of an overconfident age, a secular doctrine of progress (albeit with Christian roots), and his own essentially sunny disposition.[45]

It should not be supposed, however, that Hodge's buoyancy was the result of a trouble-free life. Quite the contrary. His father died when he was six months old, so that he was raised by his mother who had only moderate means. He was virtually confined to his house for a decade in middle life with a painful thigh ailment. His beloved first wife died when he was in his early fifties. He had the usual middle class financial worries.[46] But, perhaps saddest of all, and something mercifully passed over in the biography of him by his son, were the family troubles which darkened his very last years, after his *Systematic Theology* had been brought forth. There were the predictable health problems of a septuagenarian and the reports of the deaths of long-time friends. But there was also the upsetting marriage of Hodge's daughter to his aged colleague, and worst of all, the morphine addiction which brought about the early death of Charles Hodge, Jr.[47] Thus, beneath the seemingly placid surface of the life of the much honored Princeton theologian was a fair share of suffering. His was no untested optimism.

Hodge's hopeful spirit leads him to believe not only that the elect comprise an innumerable host[48] but that the total number of the saved greatly exceeds the total number of the lost. He offers two principal reasons for this confidence: 1) all who die in infancy are saved, and at least half of the human race has died in infancy; and 2) while in the past only a minority of adults have been saved (cf. Matthew 7:14), the future is bright with the millennial hope that all men will know God. As early as 1824 he asserts that

> as to mere numbers there is reason to hope that the proportion of the human race which shall be ultimately lost to that which shall constitute the triumph and glory of Christ will be as the inmates of a prison to the inhabitants of a virtuous community. For few as have been the number of the pious in ages past there is a period we trust advancing when all shall know the Lord and of the ages that are past if all infants are saved as we confidently hope as half mankind die in infancy—more than half shall swell the triumphs of the Redeemer when he comes to be admired in his Saints.[49]

For over half a century he never wavered in this conviction, which he expresses in the last article he ever wrote.[50] Turretin does not appear to have speculated on the number of the elect, and Hodge might have done well to imitate him.[51] If Hodge's confidence that the knowledge of God in Christ will cover the earth displays the evangelical side of his optimism, his teaching that all those dying in infancy are saved reveals the humanistic side of his optimism.

In affirming that no dying infants are lost, Hodge means that no one is condemned to hell for original sin apart from actual sin. Infants are sinners prior to overt sin; therefore they must be saved by Christ and regenerated by the Holy Spirit.

> we have every reason to believe and hope that no human being ever actually perishes who does not personally incur the penalty of the law by his actual transgression. This however is through the redemption of Christ. All who die in infancy are doubtless saved, but they are saved by grace . . . The Reformed Churches . . . do not teach that the first sin of Adam is the single and immediate ground of the condemnation of his posterity to eternal death, but that it is the ground of their forfeiture of the divine favour from which flows the loss of original righteousness and corruption of our whole nature, which in their turn become the proximate ground of exposure to final perdition, from

which, however, as almost all Protestants believe, all are saved who have no other sins to answer for.[52]

This is a clear departure from Turretin, who repudiates such "Remonstrant" ideas.[53] It is also a plain break with the Westminster Confession, although Hodge denies that it is.[54] But many Protestant theologians—some of them anything but "old Calvinists"—can be reckoned among those who hold that all who die in infancy are ipso facto saved. In fact, nineteenth-century American Presbyterian and Protestant sentiment appears to have been fairly unanimously with Hodge on this point.[55]

Having reviewed Hodge's postmillennialism, his missionary concern, and his belief that there are more saved than lost—all points of difference with the pessimistic Turretin—it only remains for us to glance briefly at Hodge's relation to social reform and the American civil religion, both frequent accompaniments of postmillennialism in the United States in the nineteenth century.[56] Suffice it to say, that both he and his Princeton Seminary colleagues usually took a middle position between advocacy of the progressive social programs (such as abolition) frequently associated with postmillennialists like Charles G. Finney and Jonathan Blanchard, on the one hand, and virtually total disengagement from "worldly" affairs characteristic of premillennialists like Dwight L. Moody, on the other hand. Simply because Hodge and Princeton Seminary were conservative in their approach to social questions does not mean that they had no interest in improving society.[57] Moreover, like almost all of his compatriots, Hodge believed that the United States was God's appointed agent to bring civil and religious liberty to the world; and freedom of religion, of course, would foster the impending millennial blessings: thus the United States might well be said to play an indirect role in Hodge's optimistic eschatology.[58]

Finally, the foregoing essay raises certain issues. First, and perhaps most importantly, how does the authority of Scripture function in diverse cultural settings? Turretin and Hodge agree on their formal theory of biblical inspiration, but they differ significantly in their reading of biblical eschatology—and this difference seems to stem from their diverse situations and, possibly, personalities. How can we, in our time, guard against treating Scripture like the proverbial wax nose which can be twisted in almost any way to fit the dominant cultural mood? And to what degree does God work through cultural diversity in bringing his Word to us?

Second, Hodge's apparent ignorance of his significant departures from the older Reformed orthodoxy as represented by Turretin suggests that Hodge had a "tin ear" with regard to historical development. This may be true of much of American Protestant theology (John W. Nevin, Hodge's frequent theological antagonist, was an exception). Can Protestants work out a theory of doctrinal development and "tradition" which will be true to sola scriptura and at the same time avoid what the Reformation discerned as the errors of Roman Catholic traditionalism?[59]

Third, is there a way of combining the post-, pre-, and amillennial perspectives into one really "biblical" view of the future? Or must we continue to be divided by our eschatological opinions—or move in cycles on a sort of millennial roller coaster, shifting from view to view, depending on historical circumstances? This has importance also for our approach to social questions, because American Protestants today are divided to some extent between the amillennial (or postmillennial) progressive social reformers, on the one hand, and the premillennial social conservatives or non-participants, on the other hand (some of whom, however, have adopted the American civil religion; e.g., Jerry Falwell). Can and ought the "great reversal" (from evangelical social engagement to the disengagement which accompanied the rise of dispensational premillennialism about a century ago) be reversed?

A Bibliography of Works by John W. Beardslee III

I. Books

"Theological Development at Geneva Under Francis and Jean-Alphonse Turretin (1648-1737)." Ph.D. dissertation, Yale University, 1957.

Reformed Dogmatics: Seventeenth-Century Reformed Theology through the Writings of Wollebius, Voetius, and Turretin, editor and translator. Grand Rapids: Wm. B. Eerdmans Co., 1984.

Vision From the Hill, editor. Grand Rapids: Wm. B. Eerdmans Co., 1984.

II. Articles contained in books

"The Reformed Church and the American Revolution." *Piety and Patriotism,* James W. Van Hoeven, editor. Grand Rapids: Wm. B. Eerdmans Co., 1986.

III. Articles in *The Church Herald*

"Martin Luther King: 1929-1968." April 19, 1968.
"Should We Abolish Capital Punishment?" January 27, 1967.
"The Church's Mission in the World." October 28, 1966.
"Communism in Today's World and Tomorrow's." April 19, 1963.
"Who's Against Communism?" April 20, 1962.
"Responsible Action Against Communism." May 25, 1962.
"Who Cannot Go Home Again." August 5, 1960.
"The Bible and Human Rights." May 26, 1961.

IV. Articles in *The Reformed Review*

"Theocracy in Today's World: Some Considerations Regarding Marxism, Islam, and Zionism." Vol. 34, Winter 1981.
"Some Implications for Worship in Traditional Reformed Doctrine." Vol. 30, Spring 1977.

"John Henry Livingston and the Rise of American Mission Theology." Vol. 29, Winter 1976.

"Historical Response (to 'Need and Promise of Reformed Preaching')." Vol. 28, Winter 1975.

"Christian Witness Through Social Action." Vol. 24, Autumn 1970.

"Secularization." Vol. 22, Spring 1969.

V. Other articles

"Self Esteem and Sin." *Perspectives*. Vol. 1, Number 9, 1986.

"Dutch Reformed Church and the American Revolution." *Journal of Presbyterian History*. Vol. 54, Spring 1976.

"Among the Thorns: Samuel M. Zwemer." *Princeton Seminary Bulletin*. Vol. 10, June 1967.

"First Impressions." *Neglected Arabia*. Vol. 179, April-September 1937.

Notes

Chapter 2 - *Advocacy for Social Justice*

1. Jerome De Jong, "Social Concerns," in *Piety and Patriotism,* ed. by James W. Van Hoeven (Grand Rapids: Wm. B. Eerdmans Publ. Co., 1976).
2. Edward Tanjore Corwin, *A Digest of Constitutional and Synodical Legislation of the Reformed Church in America* (New York: Board of Publication of the Reformed Church in America, 1906), p. iv.
3. Unidentified quote of A. J. Muste, cited in the May 1983 issue of *Sojourners.*

Chapter 3 - *Reformed Perspectives on War and Peace*

1. *The Acts and Proceedings of the General Synod, Reformed Church in America,* 1981, p. 67. (Hereafter cited as *Minutes,* General Synod.) Subsequent references to the *Acts and Proceedings* of synod will be noted in the text by year and page number.
2. Roland Bainton, *Christian Attitudes Toward War and Peace* (New York: Abingdon Press, 1960), p. 14.
3. John Yoder, *Nevertheless* (Scottdale, PA: Herald Press, 1976).
4. Quoted by Bainton, *Christian Attitudes,* p. 73.
5. Yoder, *Nevertheless,* p. 21.
6. Bainton, *Christian Attitudes,* pp. 95-99.
7. Quoted by Bainton, Ibid., p. 97.
8. See also the discussion in Ernest Ruede, *The Morality of War* (Rome: Modrante R. P. J. O'Riordan, CSSR, 1972), p. 58.
9. Bainton, *Christian Attitudes,* p. 145.
10. Owen Chadwick, *The Reformation* (Baltimore: Penguin Books, 1964), pp. 168-70.
11. Ibid., p. 170. See also Henry Kamen, *The Rise of Toleration* (New York: McGraw-Hill Book Co., 1967), p. 148.
12. Chadwick, *The Reformation,* p. 169.
13. Bainton, *Christian Attitudes,* p. 148.

14. For a further discussion of this see John P. Luidens, *The Americanization of the Dutch Reformed Church* (Norman, OK: John P. Luidens, 1969), pp. 98-244.
15. Ibid., p. 200.
16. Yoder, *Nevertheless*, p. 34ff.
17. Ibid., p. 37-38.
18. Ruede, *The Morality of War*, p. 57.

Chapter 4 - Synodical Opposition to Apartheid

1. John W. Beardslee III, "First Impressions," *Neglected Arabia* 179 (April 1 - Sept. 1937), p. 10.
2. Beth Spring, "The Rationalization of Racism," *Christianity Today* (Oct. 4, 1985), p. 18.
3. Alan Paton, *Cry, The Beloved Country* (New York: Charles Scribner's Sons, 1948), p. xvii.
4. This information has been condensed from Fact Sheets published in cooperation with the United Nations Centre Against Apartheid, Broadway, N.Y., N.Y., 1984, p. 198.
5. *Minutes*, General Synod, 1950, p. 117. Hereafter references to General Synod Minutes will be noted in the text by year and page number.
6. W. A. Landman, *A Plea For Understanding—A Reply to the Reformed Church in America*, published by the Information Bureau of the Dutch Reformed Church in South Africa, 1968.
7. Executive Council of the NGK (editors), *Human Relations and the South African Scene in the Light of Scripture* (Cape Town, 1976).
8. Edward Tanjore Corwin, *A Digest of Constitutional and Synodical Legislation of the Reformed Church in America* (New York: Board of Publications, 1906), pp. 681-84.
9. Ibid., pp. 682-83.
10. Ibid., p. 683 (*Minutes*, General Synod, p. 1131).
11. Paton, *Beloved Country*, p. xvii.
12. *Human Relations*, p. 6.
13. Desmond Tutu, "Apartheid and Christianity," in *Apartheid is a Heresy*, ed. John W. de Gruchy and Charles Villa-Vicencio (Grand Rapids: Wm. B. Eerdmans Publ. Co., 1983), p. 40.
14. *Human Relations*, p. 14.
15. Also see *Human Relations*, sec. 9.
16. *Human Relations*, sec. 56.
17. Ibid., p. 98.

Chapter 5 - Origins of the Theological Library

1. For further information on the colonial Reformed Church see Gerald F. De Jong, *The Dutch Reformed Church in the American Colonies* (Grand Rapids: Wm. B. Eerdmans Publ. Co., 1978); James W. Van Hoeven, *Piety and Patriotism* (Grand Rapids: Wm. B. Eerdmans Publ. Co., 1976); *Centennial of the Theological Seminary of the Reformed Church in America, 1784-1884* (New York: Board of Publication, R.C.A., 1885); and Edward T. Corwin, *A Manual of the Reformed Church in America, 1628-1902* (Fourth edition; New York: Board of Publication, R.C.A., 1902).

2. See William Henry Steele Demarest, *A History of Rutgers College, 1766 to 1924* (New Brunswick: Rutgers College, 1924) and Richard P. McCormick, *Rutgers: A Bicentennial History* (New Brunswick: Rutgers University Press, 1966).

3. *Minutes*, General Synod. Hereafter the references will be cited after the passage in the body of the paper. Numbers will refer to the year and page.

4. For political affiliations and general background regarding the Dutch activity in the Revolutionary War see John W. Beardslee III, "The Reformed Church and the American Revolution," in Van Hoeven, *Piety and Patriotism*, and Adrian C. Leiby, *The Revolutionary War in the Hackensack Valley* (New Brunswick: Rutgers University Press, 1962).

5. John C. Van Dyke, "The Sage Library," *New Brunswick Theological Seminary Bulletin*, Vol. VI, No. 1, April 1931, p. 7.

6. Van Dyke, "Notes on the Sage Library," pamphlet published in New Brunswick, 1888, p. 5.

7. Information taken from Van Dyke's descriptions in his pamphlets and from personal observation of the building.

8. Information was abstracted from the catalog descriptions of the seminary regarding the library and the reports of the Board of Superintendents to the General Synod. Various sources were compared and this compilation was determined.

9. Van Dyke, "Notes on the Sage Library," p. 3.

10. W. H. S. Demarest, "John Charles Van Dyke," *New Brunswick Seminary Bulletin*, Vol. VIII, No. 1, March 1933 (Memorial Number), p. 3.

11. Edward T. Corwin, *The Ecclesiastical Records of the State of New York*, 7 volumes (Albany: J. B. Lyon, 1901-16).

Chapter 6 - From Calvin to Van Raalte

1. Quoted by E. Harris Harbison in *The Age of Reformation* (Ithaca: Cornell University Press, 1955), p. 76.
2. Albert Hyma's definitive work on the Brethren was published in 1950, *The Brethren of the Common Life* (Grand Rapids: Wm. B. Eerdmans Publ. Co., 1950).
3. John T. McNeill, *The History and Character of Calvinism* (New York: Oxford University Press, 1954), p. 255.
4. Harbison, *Age of Reformation*, p. 60.
5. Pieter Geyl, *The Revolt of the Netherlands 1555-1609* (London: Ernest Binn Limited, 1958 2nd ed.), p. 80.
6. Arthur C. Cochrane, ed., *Reformed Confessions of the 16th Century* (Philadelphia: The Westminster Press, 1966), p. 186.
7. John Patrick Donnelly, *Calvinism and Scholasticism in Vermigli's Doctrine of Man and Grace* (Leiden: E. J. Brill, 1976), p. 185.
8. Bard Thompson, "The Historical Background of the Catechism," in *Essays on the Heidelberg Catechism* (Philadelphia: United Church Press, 1963), p. 24.
9. Donnelly, *Calvinism and Scholasticism*, p. 186.
10. Hendrikus Berkhof, "The Catechism in Historical Context," in *Essays On the Heidelberg Catechism* (Philadelphia: United Church Press, 1963), p. 83.
11. G. D. J. Schotel, "A Brief History of the Heidelberg Catechism in the Netherlands," in *Tercentenary Monument* (Chambersburg, Pa.: M. Kieffer & Co., 1863), p. 164.
12. Thomas De Witt, "The Heidelberg Catechism in the Reformed Church of Holland and America," in *Tercentenary Monument*, p. 420.
13. Harbison, *Age of Reformation*, p. 118.
14. Ibid., p. 131.
15. Geyl, *Revolt*, p. 131.
16. Quoted by Carl Bangs in *Arminius: A Study in the Dutch Reformation* (Nashville: Abingdon Press, 1971), p. 220.
17. Ibid., p. 221.
18. Ibid., p. 341.
19. McNeill, *History and Character of Calvinism*, p. 265.
20. Donnelly, *Calvinism and Scholasticism*, p. 21.
21. Ibid., p. 8.

22. John W. Beardslee, *Reformed Dogmatics: Seventeenth-Century Reformed Theology through the Writings of Wollebius, Voetius, and Turretin* (New York: Oxford University Press, 1965), p. 317.

23. *Memoirs of the Rev. John Henry Livingston, D.D., First Professor of Theology in the Reformed Protestant Dutch Church in North-America* (New York: Board of Publication of the Reformed Protestant Dutch Church, 1850), p. 78.

24. For much of this section I am deeply indebted to the superb doctoral thesis of Dr. Gerrit ten Zythoff, *The Netherlands Reformed Church: Step-mother of Michigan Pioneer Albertus Christian Van Raalte* (Chicago: University of Chicago, 1968).

25. Ibid., p. 72.

26. Ibid., p. 230.

27. My great, great-grandfather Hendrik Bruins, who had a conventicle meet in his farm home near Twello, three miles from Deventer, was charged with violating Article 291 by allowing an assembly in his home without the permission of the authorities. A copy of the court action concerning him was found in Amsterdam by Dr. Cornelius Smits and is in my possession. The court did not press charges and Bruins was exonerated.

28. See my article in the *Reformed Review*, 30 (Winter 1977), pp. 83-94, which details this development in Holland, Michigan.

29. See Gordon J. Spykman, *Pioneer Preach: Albertus C. Van Raalte. A Study of His Sermon Notes* (Grand Rapids: Printed Privately, 1976).

30. "The Van Raalte Sermons," *Reformed Review*, 30 (Winter 1977), p. 98.

31. Ibid., p. 100.

32. The Free University was located originally at Keizergracht 162 but has relocated to a section of suburban Amsterdam called Buitenveldert.

33. I brought back with me copies of this correspondence when I returned from my sabbatical in the Netherlands in 1973.

Chapter 7 - From Pessimism to Optimism

1. John Walter Beardslee III, "Theological Development at Geneva under Francis and Jean-Alphonse Turretin (1648-1737)," Ph.D. thesis, Yale University, 1957. Beardslee's dissertation contains some references to Charles Hodge, for

purposes of comparison with the two Turretins. See also John
W. Beardslee III, editor and translator, *Reformed Dogmatics:
Seventeenth-Century Reformed Theology through the Writings
of Wollebius, Voetius, and Turretin* (New York: Oxford
University Press, 1965), pp. 335-459. Also John W. Beardslee
II, ed., Francis Turretin, *The Doctrine of Scripture: Locus 2 of
Institutio Theologiae Elencticae* (Grand Rapids: Baker Book
House, 1981).

2. Earl William Kennedy, "An Historical Analysis of Charles
   Hodge's Doctrines of Sin and Particular Grace," Th.D thesis,
   Princeton Theological Seminary, 1968. Hodge boasted at the
   end of his theological career that "no new idea" had ever been
   taught at Princeton Seminary, and most of both his admirers
   and detractors have taken him at his word. My thesis was that
   Hodge was mistaken in his statement, and that Princeton
   Seminary in general and Hodge in particular had adapted the
   seventeenth-century heritage (for example, Francis Turretin,
   whom they claimed to follow) in significant ways to
   nineteenth-century American conditions. See Mark A. Noll,
   ed. and compiler, *The Princeton Theology 1812-1921:
   Scripture, Science, and Theological Method from Archibald
   Alexander to Benjamin Warfield* (Grand Rapids: Baker Book
   House, 1983), p. 39. Francis Turretin, incidentally, was widely
   popular in orthodox Presbyterian and Reformed circles in the
   eighteenth and nineteenth centuries in both Europe and
   America.

3. An examination of the educational histories of the presidents
   of the General Synod of the Reformed Church in America
   from 1835 to 1955 shows that about eighteen of these men had
   attended or graduated from Princeton Seminary in the time of
   Hodge and of his like-minded predecessors and successors.
   Peter N. VandenBerge, *Historical Directory of the Reformed
   Church in America 1628-1978* (Grand Rapids: Wm. B.
   Eerdmans Publ. Co., 1978), p. 345f. Furthermore, of the
   professors of systematic theology at New Brunswick Seminary,
   Joseph F. Berg (1861-71) was a theological ally of Hodge,
   Abraham Brooks Van Zandt (1872-81) was a Princeton
   Seminary graduate and student of Hodge, and John Preston
   Searle (1893-1922) was a student of Van Zandt. More
   significantly, although the late nineteenth-century and early
   twentieth-century New Brunswick Seminary catalogs do not
   reveal the English language textbooks used for systematic

theology, they do indicate that long-time professor Samuel M. Woodbridge's *Analysis of Theology* was used around the turn of the century. In a copy of this work once owned by A. Livingston Warnshuis (dated by him April 26, 1898), now in the Gardner Sage Library at New Brunswick Seminary, Warnshuis records the collateral reading assignments in ink. These numerous references (and sometimes quotations) are largely to pages of Hodge's *Systematic Theology.* Finally, an examination of the Western Seminary catalogs in this same time period shows that Hodge's three-volume textbook was the chief work assigned from 1889 to 1913. Later catalogs do not indicate which systematic theology texts were used. See also Eugene Heideman, "Theology," in James W. Van Hoeven, ed., *Piety and Patriotism* (Grand Rapids: Wm. B. Eerdmans Publ. Co., 1976), pp. 102-6.

4. Beardslee, "Theological Development," pp. 293-95, 303f., especially 307-12, and 722; also John W. Beardslee III, "John Henry Livingston and the Rise of American Mission Theology," *Reformed Review*, vol. 29, no. 2 (Winter 1976), pp. 103-5. He sees the big difference here between Turretin and Hodge as that the former represented a Calvinism which had lost its sense of mission, while the latter had recovered it.

5. David E. Holwerda, "Eschatology and History: A Look at Calvin's Eschatological Vision" in Holwerda, David E., ed., *Exploring the Heritage of John Calvin* (Grand Rapids: Baker, 1976), pp. 110-39 (especially pp. 127-39).

6. The pursuit of a future earthly millennium was made respectable among scholars in the first half of the seventeenth century by such Reformed theologians as Johann Heinrich Alsted on the continent and Joseph Mede in England. Paul Christianson, *Reformers and Babylon: English Apocalyptic Visions from the Reformation to the Eve of the Civil War* (Toronto: University of Toronto Press, 1978), p. 129. Mystical quietism was represented by a figure such as Jean de Labadie in the Netherlands.

7. See Brian G. Armstrong, *Calvinism and the Amyraut Heresy: Protestant Scholasticism and Humanism in Seventeenth-Century France* (Madison, Wis.: University of Wisconsin Press, 1969).

8. Franciscus Turrettinus, *Institutio Theologiae Elencticae*, 3 vols. (Geneva: Samuel de Tournes, 1679-85); XII.iv.11.vi.

9. Ibid., XII.vi.5-6.

10. Ibid., I.iv.2. The nineteenth-century manuscript translation of Turretin's *Institutio* done by George Musgrave Giger of Princeton (in Speer Library, Princeton Theological Seminary) is used throughout.
11. Ibid., I.iv.5.
12. Ibid., XII.vi.11.
13. Ibid., XII.vi.14. The Canons of Dort at least give lip service to the goal of evangelizing the world; Turretin offers only excuses. In the *Institutio*, he deals with the Great Commission passage (Matthew 28:19) about a dozen times and only once does he see it as anything approaching a missionary text; *Institutio*, XIX.xii.3. He thinks, however, that shipwrecked Christians should tell their pagan hosts about Christ; XVIII.xxiii.18.
14. Stephen Neill, *Christian Missions* (The Pelican History of the Church, vol. 6; n.p., 1964), pp. 220-25.
15. He teaches the *syllogismus practicus*; *Institutio*, XXII.vi.31.
16. Ibid., XX.iv.9-12. Gerrit Keizer, *Francois Turrettine: Sa vie et ses oeuvres et le Consensus* (Kampen, The Netherlands: J. A. Bos, 1900), p. 45. There is to be no national political restoration of the Jews, however; XX.iv.13f. Johannes Coccejus (1603-69), by means of his apocalyptic expectation of the coming springtime of missions, strongly aided the Jewish mission in the Netherlands. J. Moltman, "Coccejus (Coch), Johannes," *Evangelisches Kirchenlexicon*, I (1956), columns 802-3.
17. *Institutio*, XX.iii.2f.,8; iv.5,8f.,17; xii.4. Other references to the church's present plight: III.i.3; XII.iii.14; XX.xii.6. Beardslee, in his dissertation, pp. 295, 308f., is not overly impressed with Turretin's moanings and thinks that his expressed hope of the imminent return of Christ is just a pious cliche. Cf. *Westminster Confession*, XXXIII.3.
18. *Institutio*, XV.i.5-7; ii. For preaching intentionally directed only at people in the covenant and not to the outsiders present, note what Edmund S. Morgan calls Puritan "tribalism": *The Puritan Family* (rev. ed.; New York: Harper & Row, 1966), pp. 161-86.
19. This is the main thrust of my doctoral dissertation cited in note 2 above.
20. For example, J. F. Maclear, "New England and the Fifth Monarchy: The Quest for the Millennium in Early American Puritanism," *William and Mary Quarterly*, 3rd series, vol. 32, no. 2 (April 1975), 223-60.

21. George M. Marsden, *Fundamentalism and American Culture: The Shaping of Twentieth-Century Evangelicalism: 1870-1925* (New York: Oxford University Press, 1980), p. 49f.

22. Earl William Kennedy, "From Providence to Civil Religion: Some 'Dutch' Reformed interpretations of America in the Revolutionary Era," *Reformed Review*, vol. 29, no. 2 (Winter 1976), 111-23. Beardslee, "John Henry Livingston," pp. 104-8. Later, anti-premillennialism was represented at New Brunswick Seminary by Joseph F. Berg and Samuel M. Woodbridge. Joseph F. Berg, *The Second Advent of Jesus Christ, Not Premillennial* (Philadelphia: Perkinpine & Higgins, 1859); Samuel M. Woodbridge, *Analysis of Systematic Theology* (2nd ed.; New Brunswick, 1883).

23. Marsden, *Fundamentalism*, pp. 49-51.

24. Ibid., pp. 85-93. Timothy P. Weber, *Living in the Shadow of the Second Coming: American Premillennialism 1875-1982* (rev. ed., Grand Rapids: Zondervan, 1983).

25. Charles Hodge, *Systematic Theology*, II (New York: Charles Scribner & Company, 1871), pp. 557f., 641-53.

26. Ibid., II:642.

27. Ibid., II:642f.

28. Ibid., II:643.

29. Ibid., II:643-45.

30. Ibid., I (1871):24-31, 97; II:154, 245, 364f., 646-49, 665; III (1872):468f. Hodge offers no hope for a second chance after death. See III:868ff.

31. Ibid., I:97; II:646; III:468f.

32. Ibid., I:31; II:648f.

33. A perusal of the seminary catalogs and alumni directories shows this. A. A. Hodge, *The Life of Charles Hodge D.D. LL.D.* (New York: Charles Scribner's Sons, 1880), p. 367f.

34. For example see Hodge, *Theology*, II:363, 377; III:86, 800-805; also Charles Hodge, *Conference Papers* (New York: Charles Scribner's Sons, 1879), pp. 322-29.

35. Hodge, *Theology*, III:790-92, 825, 844; *Romans Commentary*, p. 374; also Charles Hodge's "Introduction" to James B. Ramsey, *The Spiritual Kingdom: An Exposition of the First Eleven Chapters of the Book of Revelation* (Richmond, Va.: Presbyterian Committee of Publication, 1873), i-xxxv. The anti-modernist alliance of dispensationalism and Princeton theology, which began shortly after Hodge left the scene, could not have been based on similar eschatologies. It may have

been founded on a common doctrine of biblical authority, as Ernest R. Sandeen suggests in *The Roots of Fundamentalism* (Chicago: University of Chicago Press, 1970).

36. Hodge, *Theology*, III:792, 800-36, 866. Also see Hodge, *Romans Commentary*, pp. 344-82.

37. This is to say that Hodge's treatment of the doctrine of the Antichrist is academic and not particularly vivid. Perhaps one reason for this, other than Hodge's natural optimism, is that he does not regard the Roman pontiff (or even the papacy in general) to be the only Antichrist. See Hodge, *Theology*, III:822, 830. Hodge's thought at this point appears to reflect the movement away from the Westminster Confession's doctrine of the pope as the Antichrist (XXV.6). The movement culminated in the removal of that reference in the 1903 revision of the confession.

38. Turretin expresses greater interest in the conversion of the Jews (note the dispensationalists' similar concern) than Hodge does, while Hodge evinces greater interest in the conversion of the Gentiles than Turretin does. With respect to the Jews, Hodge, like Turretin, is careful to reject the (premillennial) notion that they will be restored to their homeland. Hodge excuses the missionary negligence of the earlier Protestants on the grounds that they were too busy fighting Rome, the state, and each other. Hodge, *Theology*, III:800-812.

39. Furthermore, in opposing premillennialism, Hodge does not borrow Turretin's argument about the necessity of the church's suffering in this life; nor does Hodge introduce the distinction between the church militant and the church triumphant; is this because the church's militance has made it sufficiently triumphant on earth to render the old distinction meaningless?

40. Hodge, *Theology*, III:858. There is some brief mention of these pessimistic signs in Hodge's treatment of the doctrine of the Antichrist; Ibid., III:812, 827; also see, III:799, 867.

41. Ibid., III:858f.

42. Ibid., III:822.

43. Charles Augustus Briggs, *Whither? A Theological Question for the Times* (New York: Charles Scribner's Sons, 1889), p. 206; see pp. 200-206.

44. Hodge, *Theology*, III:867f.; Hodge, *Conference Papers*, p. 67. "The world under the influence of Christianity is constantly improving, and will ultimately attain under the reign of Christ,

millennial perfection and glory"; Ibid., II:94. Here it sounds as if Christ is to bring in the millennium in person.

45. Hodge was, in his own eyes, an optimist; Charles Hodge to Hugh Lenox Hodge, April 19, 1869 (manuscript letter in Hodge Family Papers in Firestone Library, Princeton University).

46. A. A. Hodge, *Life of Hodge*, pp. 234-44; William S. Barker, "The Social Views of Charles Hodge: A Study in 19th Century Calvinism and Conservatism," *Presbyterian*, vol. I., no. 1 (Spring 1985), pp. 17-18.

47. Several manuscript letters of the year 1875 written by Hodge and his sons discuss these matters. See Hodge Family Papers in Firestone Library, Princeton University. A fresh critical biography of Charles Hodge is badly needed. Unfortunately, Lefferts A. Loetscher's projected definitive history of Princeton Seminary was never completed.

48. For example, see Hodge, *Theology*, II:320, 333, 362, 366, 547; also *Romans Commentary*, pp. 182, 191.

49. Charles Hodge, "Lectures on the Romans, Chapter V," dated January 1824, in Hodge Family Papers. Although Hodge does not say this, it may be inferred that the advance of the missionary enterprise in bringing adults to salvation will more than offset any decrease in heaven's growth brought about by the progress of medicine in reducing the infant mortality rate; Hodge, *Theology*, I:26, 29; Ibid., II:648; III:744.

50. Charles Hodge, "Institutions, and Views of Future Punishment," *The New York Evangelist*, May 9, 1878, reprinted in *The Presbyterian*, September 27, 1879 (under the title "A Last Word"), p. 5.

51. Hodge, however, was by no means alone in his teaching on this subject. Among his contemporaries, William G. T. Shedd, *Dogmatic Theology* (New York: Charles Scribner's Sons, 1888-94), II:712, 746f., III:169-71. Also see Henry B. Smith, *Introduction to Christian Theology* (New York: A. C. Armstrong, 1897), p. 230. Smith shares Hodge's view that there are more saved than lost.

52. Hodge, *Theology*, II:211f.

53. Ibid., IX.x.3,5; cf. V.viii.17.

54. Ibid., X.3; VI.6. This was one of Hodge's more flagrant historical blunders; he actually claimed that neither the Westminster Confession nor any "Calvinistic theologian" he knew held that only some of those who die in infancy are

saved; Ibid., *Theology*, III:605n. Benjamin B. Warfield in "The Development of the Doctrine of Infant Salvation," in *Two Studies in the History of Doctrine* (New York: Christian Literature Co., 1897), p. 219, virtually concedes Hodge's error here.

55. For example, John H. Livingston, Nathaniel W. Tayler, Lyman Beecher, Robert J. Breckinridge, Henry B. Smith, William G. T. Shedd, Augustus H. Strong, Archibald Alexander, A. A. Hodge, and B. B. Warfield. See Kennedy, "An Historical Analysis," p. 262f.

56. Turretin was a good Genevan patriot with a deep love for his city. See the introduction to his *Institutio*. He was less at the center of Geneva's "secular" life than was Calvin.

57. Barker, "Social Views," pp. 1-22; Earl William Kennedy, "William Brenton Greene's Treatment of Social Issues," *Journal of Presbyterian History*, vol. 40 (1962), pp. 92-112; David Murchie, "Charles Hodge and Jacksonian Economics," *Journal of Presbyterian History*, vol. 61 (1983), pp. 248-56. Marsden, *Fundamentalism*, pp. 85-93, on the "Great Reversal"; pp. 124-38 on four views of Christianity and culture ca. 1910. Weber, *Second Coming*, deals with premillennial dispensationalism's relation to "the world" throughout his study. The alliance of Princetonians and dispensationalists in the early twentieth century had nothing to do with a common attitude toward social questions.

58. Marsden, *Fundamentalism*, pp. 11-13. Hodge's patriotism was, like that of John H. Livingston, more restrained than that of some American theologians. See Ernest Lee Tuveson, *Redeemer Nation: The Idea of America's Millennial Role* (Chicago: The University of Chicago Press, 1968); also Winthrop S. Hudson, ed., *Nationalism and Religion in America: Concepts of American Identity and Mission* (New York: Harper & Row, 1970); also Conrad Cherry, ed., *God's New Israel: Religious Interpretations of American Destiny* (Englewood Cliffs, N. J.: Prentice-Hall, 1971).

59. John Henry Newman made a famous effort at interpreting and defending the development of doctrine from the Roman Catholic perspective. James Orr and, more recently, Peter Toon have attempted to do the same thing from a Protestant point of view; see Peter Toon, *The Development of Doctrine in the Church* (Grand Rapids: Wm. B. Eerdmans Publishing Co., 1979).

Index